T65

✠✠✠✠✠✠✠✠✠✠✠✠✠✠✠✠✠✠✠✠✠✠✠✠✠✠

This Book is presented to

JAMES ALAN SCHUMACHER

by the Board of Christian Education
of the Presbyterian Church in the U.S.A.

It is one of many means by which the
Church serves her ministers and teachers
in the work of the Kingdom.

✠✠✠✠✠✠✠✠✠✠✠✠✠✠✠✠✠✠✠✠✠✠✠✠✠✠

WHICH BOOKS
Belong
IN THE BIBLE?

Books by Floyd V. Filson
Published by The Westminster Press

OPENING THE NEW TESTAMENT
ONE LORD, ONE FAITH
WHICH BOOKS BELONG IN THE BIBLE?

In Collaboration with G. Ernest Wright
THE WESTMINSTER HISTORICAL ATLAS TO THE BIBLE
(Revised)

WHICH BOOKS
Belong
IN THE BIBLE?

A Study of the Canon

by FLOYD V. FILSON

PHILADELPHIA
THE WESTMINSTER PRESS

Library of Congress Catalog Card Number: 57–6289

PRINTED IN THE UNITED STATES OF AMERICA

Contents

Preface

The purpose of this book is not to trace the outward process by which the books in our Bible were tested, collected, and recognized as Scripture. That task is well done in books listed in the bibliography. My aim has been rather to consider whether the Church should have a Scripture, what books should be included in it, and why. These are theological issues, and I have tried to give a clear discussion of them.

The following pages present in revised form the L. P. Stone Lectures delivered April 9 to 12, 1956, at Princeton Theological Seminary. I am grateful to President John A. Mackay and the faculty of the seminary for the invitation to give these lectures. I wish also to express my deep appreciation to President and Mrs. Mackay, the faculty, the students, and friends of the seminary for the gracious hospitality and unfailing courtesy which my wife and I received during our stay on the Princeton campus.

Floyd V. Filson

July 20, 1956

7

I

Why Study the Canon?

DOES the Church need a Bible? Does the Bible we have contain exactly the right books? Most Christians never ask such questions. They take it for granted that the Church must have the Bible in the form they know. They assume that the list of books to be included is definitely fixed and need not be discussed. The Bible exists; the Church accepts it; the Christian should use it. The matter is clear and simple.

A LONG HISTORY OF DISAGREEMENT

This attitude ignores much history and overlooks many facts. It is true that the Church has always had its Scripture. Jesus and the apostles accepted and used as inspired Scripture the collection of writings that we call the Old Testament. From that time to the present the Church has continued to give Scripture a prominent place in its worship and life. Yet never during the more than nineteen centuries of its history has the Church completely agreed as to just what the Bible should include.

When the first Christians took over the Jewish Scriptures, two important problems still called for settlement. One was the exact number of books that Jews who used the Hebrew Bible should accept in their Hebrew canon. The issue was practically decided, but debate lingered on.

9

The other difficulty was the amazing difference between
the original Hebrew text and the Greek translation which
Greek-speaking Jews used and Greek-speaking Christians
took over from them.

Echoes of the former problem were heard in the Ancient
Church and even later. The Book of Esther, for example,
was omitted by Melito of Sardis; late in the second century
he made a trip " to the east," that is, to Palestine, to find
out what books were included in the Old Testament, and
what he learned led him to omit Esther. (Eusebius, writing in the first half of the fourth century, reports this fact
in his *Church History,* Book IV, Ch. 26.) Esther was likewise denied full canonical status by the Egyptian bishop
Athanasius in A.D. 367. Martin Luther, in the early six-
teenth century, spoke with vigorous disparagement of this
and a few other Old Testament books. Yet on the whole
the Church has usually accepted the books of the Hebrew
canon without serious debate. It is the second issue, the
choice between the Hebrew canon and the larger Greek
Old Testament, that has divided the Church throughout
its history, and this is still a serious source of division.

The New Testament portion of the canon has proved
less divisive. Yet throughout the ancient and medieval
ages, and even into modern times, differences have persisted. Such spurious works as III Corinthians and Laodiceans appeared in Biblical manuscripts for many centuries. On the other hand, we find doubts expressed in the
early centuries concerning Hebrews, the Catholic Epistles,
and Revelation; the book of Revelation seems to have
aroused the most persistent protests. The Reformation period was a time of renewed debate concerning the limits of
the New Testament canon. Martin Luther was the leader
most responsible for this reconsideration, but Erasmus and
Zwingli were also prominent in the discussion.

THE QUESTION IMPORTANT FOR PROTESTANTS

The question of the limits of the canon is of particular importance for the Protestant wing of the Christian Church. This is true for two reasons. For one thing, Protestants cannot deal with this issue as Catholic groups do. The Roman Catholic Church relies on tradition and Church authority. Moreover, by definite and binding decisions it has taken a clear and final position on the canon. The Greek Church trusts tradition and liturgy so much that it feels no compulsion to settle persistent differences of opinion on this issue. Protestant groups, however, have never given to Church decisions and tradition such a dominant role. They must face the question for themselves.

In the second place, the Bible is more basic in the Protestant point of view than it is for other Christian Churches. To be sure, all Christians acknowledge the Bible as basic. But the Protestants give to the Bible the unique and unrivaled place of authority. In other branches of Christendom other bases of authority — the hierarchy of the Church, or Church tradition — are given an equal or even superior role. The Protestant, with his emphasis on the Bible, thus has particular reason to decide just what books his Bible should contain.

It may seem that to stir up the old debates on this subject will only cause needless trouble. It may be thought that even if other Christian groups do not have in their Bible the same list of books as we have in ours, we at least have made up our minds on the list we intend to use. To revive the discussion, therefore, may appear futile as well as disturbing.

Nothing could be farther from the truth. The question continually arises in the Church. Ministers may be more aware of it than the average layman. Some of them ask whether such books as Esther and the Song of Songs and Revelation really belong in the Bible. Lay church members occasionally have their questions, though they rarely feel qualified to press them. But the issue is now being raised afresh in a way that is certain to catch the attention of the English-speaking world.

THE NEW REVISION OF THE APOCRYPHA

In December, 1952, the National Council of the Churches of Christ in the U.S.A. authorized a revision of the Apocrypha, and instructed the Standard Bible Committee to undertake the work. The revision is scheduled for publication as a separate volume late in 1957, and it may be available later as part of one volume which will contain the Old Testament, the Apocrypha, and the New Testament. This revision will force the Protestant Churches to consider what books they should include in their Bible.

The publication of a revised translation of the Apocrypha may be regarded as an innovation, and it may be asked why this innovation occurs at this time. In reply to this query at least two things should be said.

In the first place, it is not such an innovation as it seems. The Apocrypha were a part of the King James Version of 1611, and were usually printed as part of that version until about one hundred and thirty years ago. Moreover, while the English Revised Version was widely considered complete in 1885, when the Old and New Testaments were published together, that version also finally included a revision of the Apocrypha; the revision was published ten years later, in 1895, for those who wanted the Bible with that addition. So the Revised Standard Version is following in the footsteps of the two great English versions that preceded it.

In the second place, the National Council of Churches

includes denominations that use passages from the Apocrypha in their cycles of Scripture readings. One of these Churches, favorable to the Revised Standard Version, proposed the revision. It naturally wanted the Revised Standard Version to contain all the passages that it uses in public worship. The intention of the new revision is to supply that need, but without forcing the Apocrypha on the churches that do not want these books in their copies of the Bible.

One fact, however, is clear. The publication of this revision of the Apocrypha immediately raises the question of the merits of these books. Are they to be included in our Scripture? Are they in a special way supplementary to Scripture? Or are they books that have no more connection with Scripture than do other valuable writings?

We therefore need to study the canon afresh. There is a particular need today to inquire what books our Church should include in the Christian Scriptures, and why.

OUTLINE OF THE FOLLOWING STUDY

We divide our discussion into five parts: (1) First of all, to give the proper background for our study, we state what we mean by the word " canon," what in broad outline the function of the canon has been, and what trends of current thought obscure or challenge the rightful authority of the Bible in the Church. (2) We then discuss the Christian view of the Old Testament. (3) Because of the sharp differences among Christians as to whether the Apocrypha should be accepted as Scripture, we next consider whether the Church should give the Apocrypha a place in the Bible. (4) Our fourth discussion deals with the apostolic witness in the New Testament; it tries to show the basis on which the New Testament was formed. (5) Last of all, since certain Christian Churches assign to their tradition a role equal to or, in effect, even higher than that given to the

Bible, we face frankly the question of the relative importance of Scripture and tradition.

Our main purpose is not to describe in detail the historical process by which the books of the Bible were collected and set apart as the canon of the Christian Church. Many aspects of that process will be noted, but our real aim is not to describe the process. It is rather to understand the thinking of the Church. We seek to understand why the Church needed the Bible, what guided the Church in forming our Bible, and what the Bible should mean to the modern Church and its members.

II

What Place Has the Canon Today?

THE MEANING OF "CANON"

THE word "canon" was a Greek word, which seems to have come from a Hebrew word meaning "reed." The word was used of an instrument made of reed or other material, and denoted especially such an instrument used as a rod or ruler, as an aid in making straight lines or accurate measurements. Thus it came to mean a standard of straightness or accuracy. In a figurative sense, it referred to rules or standards for conduct or for workmanship. Paul, the only New Testament writer to use the word, used it in Gal. 6:16 of the rule or standard of Christian living, and in II Cor. 10:13-16 of the "limit" or prescribed "field" of the Christian leader's work.

One use of the word "canon" was to describe documents which provided a standard or norm. In this connection we should note the word's use with the special meaning of a list of items or writings. It is not entirely clear whether the first use of the word "canon" to designate the books of the Bible referred primarily to the *list* of them or to the *rule* or *standard* of faith and life which they contained. It seems that neither idea could ever have been completely lacking — each was at least implied from the first — but the conviction that these books were basic and authoritative appears primary.

THE MEANING OF "CANON" FOR THE CHURCH

These writings were the books approved for regular use in the public worship and the teaching of the Church. The early use of the Old Testament in Christian worship had a background in its continual use in the Jewish synagogue. When the full Christian canon took form within the Church, it too lived on in the use of the Church. It received continual public recognition by regular public use in worship and teaching, and it received this recognition and use because it contained and gave to the Church the basic gospel message and the divine claim which gave the Church its life and mission.

Def.

The canon, then, in the Christian view, contains the writings given to the Church by the working of God. It presents his word, his gospel, his claim, and his promise. It records his Christ-centered revelation, and offers the continuous possibility of fresh Christ-centered revelation to each successive generation of the Church. It thus provides a fully dependable basis for Christian faith and worship and thought and life.

The idea of the canon relates these books to the contemporary Church. They are much more than a source of knowledge about past history. They are, of course, indispensable for the historical study of the origins of Christianity. They report the unique and decisive working of God in Israel, Christ, and the apostles. But the idea of the canon includes more than this historical reference. It includes the continuing spiritual authority of these books. They can speak with authority in every generation. They speak to the receptive hearer concerning the divine judgment, grace, and demand for obedience. The message of the Bible is God-given: it is of fundamental importance for the Church and for every Christian; it tells of that working of God on which the Church and Christian faith is founded; it is the indispensable and incomparable Book which speaks an urgently authoritative word to every generation. By this Book the Church is to be tested and the Christian is to find his standard. By it the Church is to find its way in its worship and fellowship and outreaching ministry.

But we must be still clearer as to what we mean by this message and authority of the Bible. We spoke of " the continuous possibility of fresh Christ-centered revelation." We said that these books " can speak with authority." But we did not guarantee that result. We could not. When the Bible lies unused on a shelf or table, it does not speak the word of God to the Church. Even when opened, if it is used in cynicism or derision, it has no life-changing message or power. And even when studied seriously to learn the political, social, and religious practices of the Israelites and early Christians, it is just another good book. The real work of this Book requires a special receptivity in the hearer or reader. Indeed, it requires still more. It requires a prompting, a fresh working, a direct challenge and gift from God — the same God who was active both in the story that the Bible tells and in the writing and collection of the books that it contains.

The uniqueness of the Bible, the truth of its gospel message, the authority with which it speaks, become clear not by its unaided power, nor even when aided by the best human brilliance, but only when the Spirit of God presses home to the listening congregation or the attentive reader the truth and claim of God and his gospel. This is what we call the inner witness of the Holy Spirit. We must be clear that the canon exerts no automatically effective external authority and power. Neither in worship nor in thinking nor in daily living does the Bible give us the

Word of God apart from our grateful and reverent response to the working of the Spirit of God in the Church and the Christian.

The subject of the canon, therefore, deals not only with history but also with faith and theology. It is obviously in part a historical question. These books of the Bible were written at certain times, and they tell of the men and events of certain periods. They were collected by a gradual process; they were not handed down at one time from a printing press in heaven. Neither the individual writings nor their collection to form the Bible can be understood except by serious historical study.

But the canon constitutes a challenge to faith and so presents theological issues. The word implies that God did something special in a specific history. It suggests that he was active in the production and collection of these writings. It asserts that the Bible does the work it is meant to do only when God is active in the use of the Book in the Church today. In studying the canon, therefore, we are studying theology in its characteristically Christian form. For Christian theology is always concerned with history, special history in which God is at work, history that has urgent meaning for us as we attend to it in faith and see God at work in it to fulfill his purpose.

TRENDS IN RECENT THOUGHT

If everyone agreed with these statements, there would be little need for further discussion. But the fact is that what I have said is a personal judgment, a personal confession of faith, in an area that is marked by an almost bewildering variety of views. We must consider the canon with this present situation in mind. To prepare us for the main discussions in the four chapters that follow, we need to survey some recent trends of thought as they affect the study of the canon.

1. *Indifference or Overzealous Biblicism.* Christian thought often needs to find a balance between two extreme positions, each of which is equally unsatisfactory. It is wrong to neglect a truth which is not the whole truth. But an important truth must not be discredited by an over-stress which in effect discredits it. This warning applies to our thinking about the canon. For example, we need to avoid indifference on the one hand and overzealousness on the other.

a. By indifference we do not mean complete indifference to the Christian faith or the Bible. To be sure, whoever has no interest in the Christian faith will have no real concern for the essential message of the Bible. The Bible is really the Bible, and the canon can really be an important issue, only to those who hear in these writings the Word of God. The real test of acceptance of the canon is obedience. Those who do not respond to the gospel message of the Bible certainly have no adequate sense of what the canon means. But this is not what we here mean by speaking of indifference to the canon.

There are Christians in the Church who show this indifference to the Bible. They do not mean to be evil. It is not their intent to surrender the Christian faith. But they feel that they can find God in nature or in a modern poem as well as in the Psalms or the Gospels. They do not see why they should give the Bible a unique, authoritative role which sets it quite apart from all other writings. They say, as the words of a hymn put it, that God " speaks to me everywhere." The Bible for such people is just one of many places to go for help; it is not unique; it is not decisively different from other sources of help.

Is this view wrong? Not entirely. God can speak to the Christian through nature or through a contemporary poem. But this indifference to the canon misses two points. One is that it mistakes what the Bible is for. It is not just a book to stimulate emotion, imagination, and reverence. It does that, but its ministry goes deeper. It deals with the basic situation of men before God. It faces the fact of man's failure and need. It lays bare God's complete claim on man; it shows man's inability to meet his need by himself; it speaks to him not merely in judgment but also in grace and power.

The vague worshiper misses another point. His faith and hope, if real and fruitful, root in the central historical work of God which is of radical importance for every human being. God has acted in a special history which centers in Jesus Christ. The benefit and blessing of God flow from that effective action. This gospel of God's central action is what the Bible presents, the Church preaches, and the Christian receives in faith. Once man grasps the true message of the Bible, he can never say again that his Christian faith can rest on a beautiful sunset as much as on the Biblical message of the love of God in Christ. This message of this Book must have a central place, and the Bible therefore has a basic role.

b. It is possible, however, to stress the Bible so much and give it so central a place that the sensitive Christian conscience must rebel. We may illustrate such overstress on the Bible by the often-used (and perhaps misused) quotation from Chillingworth: " The Bible alone is the religion of Protestantism." Or we may recall how often it has been said that the Bible is the final authority for the Christian.

If it will not seem too facetious, I would like to put in a good word for God. It is God and not the Bible who is the central fact for the Christian. When we speak of "the Word of God" we use a phrase which, properly used, may apply to the Bible, but it has a deeper primary meaning. It is God who speaks to man. But he does not do so only through the Bible. He speaks through prophets and apostles. He speaks through specific events. And while his unique message to the Church finds its central record and written expression in the Bible, this very reference to the Bible reminds us that Christ is the Word of God in a living, personal way which surpasses what we have even in this unique book. Even the Bible proves to be the Word of God only when the Holy Spirit working within us attests the truth and divine authority of what the Scripture says. Faith must not give to the aids that God provides the reverence and attention that belong only to God our Father and the Lord Jesus Christ. Our hope is in God; our life is in Christ; our power is in the Spirit. The Bible speaks to us of the divine center of all life and help and power, but it is not the center. The Christian teaching about the canon must not deify the Scripture.

2. *Legalism or Contempt for the Written Word.* In our study of modern views of the canon we will do well to study another pair of opposites. Christians differ in the way they react to the written word.

a. To some Christians the written record is the full, final, and binding expression of truth. It gives them definite directions for their worship and daily action. The Bible takes on the character of a rule book which tells them what to do, and they are happiest if they can find a specific instruction that appears to prescribe just what they should do in a given case. God has given men his law in the Bible, and man is to obey it literally.

Such people pay the greatest respect to the Bible. They probably would be the first to become uneasy and even indignant at any attempt to change the canon.

There is much that is deep and loyal in this attitude. It takes the claim of God seriously and sets out to do something about it. It expresses both reverence and the spirit of obedience. But it mistakes the nature of the Bible and also of the demand of God. The Bible does press home the claim of God to obedience, but it is not a book of rules. It tells the story of God's work of judgment and redemption. It offers the gospel. It calls for faith. It promises the help of the Spirit. It demands a life of love. And here is the point to remember: love cannot be reduced to law and rules. It calls for a free, responsible life of loyalty to God, in gratitude for his immense gift through Christ. Legalism is blind to the high level of the freedom and responsible privilege of the redeemed people of God.

This reminds us that God does not deal with his people by mechanical, legal, and external control. The apostle Paul, in his letter to the Galatian churches, did his utmost to make this fact clear. Fellowship with God, obedience to his will, and helpfulness to his people cannot be reduced to a legal code. The response of faith is an obedience in which the gift of the Spirit and the intelligence of the consecrated Christian are at work. They lead to a responsible decision as to what the will of God is in each situation. The infinitely varied demands of life cannot be charted and made the subject of fixed rules. The Christian is free to serve God out of gratitude; the mature Christian develops a sense of what the grace of God and the example of Christ are leading him to do. The Bible is an indispensable source of knowledge and guidance. But the acceptance of the canon does not impose a legal code of conduct on the Christian.

b. Quite opposed to legalism is the stress that some Christians put upon the Spirit. They delight to quote

Paul's word, " The written code kills, but the Spirit gives life " (II Cor. 3:6). They talk as though Paul wrote a letter to say that the written word is actually a deadly thing. With this idea that written words have no life-giving power may be coupled the hidden thought that past history is a barren concern. The active present work of the Spirit is the thing that really counts. The Christian is Spirit-guided and so is a free person; he cannot be tied to even the best of written documents.

Those who think thus have avoided the error of seeking the guidance for life in a purely external authority. They know that God must speak within them if his word is to reach and rule them; they have seen — though they exaggerate — the truth of the inner witness of the Holy Spirit. And they know that a story about a past event is not yet an effective gospel. It must go on to give meaning to life now. God deals with men in the present.

But this sweeping depreciation of all written records has serious faults. It inevitably denies the Bible any vital and indispensable place in the Church. It eliminates any need or place for the canon. Most important of all, it ignores the decisive role of God's historical work in Israel and Christ and the Apostolic Church. On this redemptive work the gospel rests. The inner witness of the Spirit must bring home this gospel to us; it must interpret the Bible to us; but the Spirit does not substitute for the historical work of God in Christ. The Spirit is rather, as the Gospel of John insists, the gift of the risen Christ, and he will recall the work and words of the ministry of Jesus and show the believer their meaning (John 14:26; 15:26; 16:7-14) .

The Holy Spirit recalls, interprets, continues, and advances the work of Jesus Christ. Thus he does not discredit or replace the historical message, and so he does not cancel the place of the written record that the Bible gives of God's work and revelation. The claim that an idea or an experience or a work is due to the Holy Spirit always has to submit to this test: Is it consistent with what God did in Christ? The canon enables the Church to make that test; the witness of the Spirit, on the other hand, keeps the Bible from being a dead letter and makes it a living power in each new day.

3. *Outgrown Product or Timeless Truth.* The time factor has produced still a third pair of opposites which demand our attention. Any view of the canon must deal with the fact that these writings come to us from ancient times. The most recent Biblical book is well over eighteen hundred years old; the oldest sections originated about three thousand years ago. Three fourths of the Bible was written more than two thousand years ago: this large portion was all written before the birth of Jesus. The New Testament writings date back more than eighteen hundred years, and since that time immense changes have affected the whole life situation of men.

a. This long period of time and the great changes it has brought make some people doubt whether writings so old can have decisive importance for us. These books come from a people and scene quite different from the life situation we know. If we were thrust back into that ancient time and situation, the sense of strangeness would no doubt overwhelm us. How can writings from such a setting speak to us with final authority?

We must couple with this sense of the antiquity and remoteness of the Biblical scene the effect of the modern idea of evolution. It points out that what is ancient is usually if not always primitive, incomplete, and imperfect. It is superseded by later developments. Notable and praiseworthy as it may have been in its day, it cannot have authority for later times. By the same logic, the greatest and best of our present wisdom can claim but a passing authority. The steadily advancing knowledge and skill of mankind will soon antiquate it.

This entire point of view is hostile to the idea of the canon. It clearly implies that no group of writings from the distant past, no matter how significant in their day, can possibly hold a permanently central and normative place. Even if our generation could produce outstanding works in the religious sphere, they could never hope to attain canonical status. The works of later writers would surely surpass them; they would soon be relegated to a place of ever diminishing importance in the long series of significant religious literature.

The truth in such a claim deserves frank recognition. The Biblical writings *are* antiquated in many ways. We do not find in them the permanently valid and final truth about scientific theory and techniques. The specific methods of government and the pattern of social organization are not today what they were then. They cannot be. There are aspects of the thinking of Biblical men that we do not continue and could not reproduce if we tried. We do not have the canon so that we may have an infallible textbook on science, government, or sociology.

But the question is whether the Bible's message from God and teaching about God is antiquated. To put it another way, does the evolutionary idea apply in the central things of religion? There is a degree of truth in the evolutionary idea even from the Christian point of view. It expresses truth concerning God's manner of creation. And in the story that the Bible tells, there is a picture of advance in the work and revelation of God. The Old Testament does not present his work and will with the clarity and power that in the fullness of time appeared in Jesus Christ. And while some may conclude from the Gospel story that everything following that appearance of Christ is necessarily anticlimactic, the Gospel of John still promises a real development in the understanding of the disciples: they will be led into truth that they have not yet learned even from Jesus himself (ch. 16:13). The gospel anticipates that the Christian individual will grow in grace and that the Church will grow in Christian understanding and faithfulness. The Christian life is not static, nor is it an anticlimactic sequel to the career of Jesus. The doctrine of the canon does not condemn the Church to a monotonous process of simply holding fast to what has been received. It agrees with the words of the Lord to Moses, " Tell the people of Israel to go forward " (Ex. 14:15).

Yet the idea of evolution is not true to the central message of the gospel. The eternal God of holiness and love does not undergo a continuous evolutionary development. It is in his very steadfastness that man finds hope. Moreover, while God deals with man at each successive stage of historical development, the history of mankind under God is not a steady, unbroken upward climb, in which each stage is a slight advance upon the preceding one. There are times when God's acts and his messengers reflect a spiritual grandeur that the next generation of sinful men does not match. And, in particular, God's work is not held in control by the spiritual qualifications and development of men. He did not choose Israel because they had achieved the greatest development in the evolutionary process. It was not their goodness that compelled him; it was his grace that chose and used them.

Most of all, the coming of Christ did not mean that Israel had now developed to so high a level that Christ was the natural expression of the achieved greatness of this people. Quite the contrary. Back of the Father's sending of his Son to bring salvation to the world was the need of

men, a need that Israel shared, so that the gospel came to
them first with its rebuke and its offer of salvation. What
God did in Christ was unique, radically decisive, and permanently central for man's faith and worship and thought
and life. No apostle thought that he was to surpass Christ.
He knew rather that he was gratefully to follow and preach
Christ the Lord; he knew that only through Christ's continuing help could he do the " greater works " of his ministry (John 14:12). Nor did any New Testament writer
consider Christ to be merely the temporary leader of men,
authoritative only until a greater leader appeared on the
scene. Christ would reign until he had " put all his enemies
under his feet " (I Cor. 15:25); he would act for God in
the final establishment of the perfect eternal Kingdom.

Here is the basis for the canon. The Bible does not tell
the story of the spiritual evolution of mankind. It tells of
God's action to realize his purpose and redeem his people
through Christ. It presents the message that must be basic
for true faith and loyalty through all the generations of
history. It gives the message that speaks with authority, demand, and promise to each succeeding generation. Because
this is so, the canon is entirely justified. It embodies the
fact that the action of God, the revelation of God, recorded
and given in this particular Book, is unique and permanently authoritative. It bars the way to a fluid, evolutionary
conception of the content of true religion.

b. There are Christians whose view is the opposite of
the evolutionary view. To them the Bible is no outmoded
historical account. It is a timeless book.

These people rightly see that the Bible presents a message of permanent validity and importance. They know
that the spiritual need of man is essentially the same in any
century. We are all akin; deep down we are the same way-
ward human beings as the psalmist who confessed his sin

or as the Pharisee or publican who heard the indictment and gracious invitation of Jesus. We may have found new ways to add frills to our sinning, but sin is just what it always was, the failure to respond gratefully and loyally to the goodness and will of God. There is thus a continually contemporary note in the Biblical message. We may have television and jet planes, but we still need the grace of God in Christ. The message of the gospel can still speak to us with direct and penetrating power. Because this is so, some prefer to think of the Bible as a timeless book.

When we compare the evolutionary view, that the Bible is a great but antiquated product of outgrown days, with this earnest affirmation that the Bible message is a timeless and ever relevant expression of basic truth, our sympathy may be with the latter view. It grasps the heart of the matter. We have not outgrown the Bible. And so the canon is a conception that we can understand and defend. But it is possible to defend a true and crucial position in a way that will discredit it in the eyes of vast numbers of people, and this sometimes happens with the Bible.

Recent centuries have seen a sorry series of attempts — they still continue — to vindicate the Bible by denying that the Bible is enmeshed in the ancient situation in any notable way. Earnest Christians declare that its science, its method of historical writing, its social practices, and its ways of thinking and teaching are all so free from antiquated features and so timeless in their nature that they are just as valid and binding today as they ever were. Or they take the Bible as a book quite detached from historical setting; they think that it teems with timeless truths which are clear without historical study.

In either form this position cannot be defended. The Bible is an ancient book; in numerous ways it reflects the transient situation in which its parts were written. That is always the case with true and effective Christian preaching, teaching, and writing. It lives in the time to which it speaks. It makes the gospel a living power in the situation in which it works. Its power is not in its freedom from the conditions of the life of its day, but in its ability to find an expression that speaks to men in terms they know and gives an effective answer to the needs they have.

The canon is not a demand that men must always think precisely as the men of Biblical times thought. It is not a demand that we accept literally the world view (or the successive world views) of the Biblical writers. But it is the claim that what God did in those ancient days was the effective answer to man's need. It was the clear and essential revelation of his work and will and nature, and this work and revelation are basic for all the future relation of man to God. Therefore these writings must always have a central place in the life of God's people. They are so important that even though the world view of later generations changes and the outward setting of life is different, the essential content of the Bible must be grasped afresh in each generation; through the worship, preaching, and teaching of the Church this Biblical message must be made a living, life-shaping power in the changed outward conditions of modern man.

It will be fatal for the Church if it fails to see the practical issues that are here involved. In many outward respects the eighth century B.C. and the first century A.D. were not like the twentieth century A.D. We must face this difference. It means that if we are to promote effective Protestant use of the Bible we must cultivate in Christians a clear historical sense. We must do this so well that Christian people can interpret the Bible rightly and apply it helpfully in our superficially different day. This creates problems in Christian education. The ages for which we have our greatest

enrollment of children in Sunday school are those in which
the child's historical sense has not yet developed. The necessity for historical understanding, however, is clear.
Therefore the Church must develop a vigorous educa-
tional program for older children, young people, and
adults.

We cannot abandon the first century gospel. In all its
essentials it is valid now as then. But we cannot make first
century Christians out of twentieth century people; we can
no more perpetuate all the outward forms of New Testament life than we can recapture and embody literally the
Old Testament setting of faith in nomadic and Israelite
times. With all honesty and without condescension we
must let those ancient people live and think in their ancient setting, and we must see God at work through them.
Then with a reverent care that preserves fully the message
of what God was doing and saying in the Biblical story,
but with a fearless readiness to preach that truth in the
shifting setting of modern life, we must pray God for grace
and power to make that gospel as persuasive and transform-
ing in our day as it proved it could be in the first century.

The doctrine of the canon does not require us to ignore
or deny the outward differences between Biblical times
and our days. It does say that we are to take the gospel and
revelation of God in the Bible as seriously today as it was
taken by the loyal members of the Apostolic Church. We
are to make the Biblical message as supreme in our faith
and life as it was in the truest Christians of the first generations. We are to know the Bible so well, and use it so effec-
tively, that regardless of the superficial changes that each
generation brings in the circumstances of life, our oneness
with the faith and dedication of the Apostolic Church will
be clear. To do this is to hold to the canon.

4. *Divine Dictation or Human Product.* Understanding

of the canon may be warped by another pair of contrasting viewpoints, each of which results from a one-sided effort to define the place of the human author in the production of the books of the Bible.

a. On the one side there is the conviction that to be worthy of canonical standing a writing must be solely the work of God. It must not be subject to the mental limitations, psychological peculiarities, and limited spiritual experience of even a great man. It must be purely and literally the word of God himself, written, as the Roman Catholic Council of Trent stated in 1546, " with the Holy Spirit dictating."

Those who study the Greek manuscripts of the New Testament are familiar with an illustration that embodies this point of view. It occurs in a number of manuscripts as a frontispiece to the Gospel of John. The Evangelist stands in the center. With one hand cupped to his ear, he listens intently to the voice of God, whose presence and speech are suggested by rays of light and a human-looking hand which extends down from a cloud at the upper corner of the picture. At the feet of the Evangelist sits his scribe, Prochorus, who writes what the Evangelist, with a gesture, repeats to him. If the Evangelist hears and speaks correctly, and Prochorus hears and writes accurately, the result is the divinely dictated Gospel of John.

This, in the view of many Christians, is the way the Biblical books should have been written. The same idea is reflected in the ancient legend concerning the origin of the Septuagint version of the Pentateuch. According to one form of an often-repeated story, seventy or seventy-two Jewish scholars were put by twos in separate cells; according to another form of the legend, each was placed alone in a separate cell. Yet the story insists that they all came out with exactly the same Greek translation of the Hebrew text. God had inspired or dictated the very words of the translation. That this legend could arise among the Jews and find repeated use in the Early Church, in spite of the fact that every chapter of the Greek Pentateuch has numerous passages that are not translated literally from the Hebrew, shows how often piety has yearned for a verbally dictated Bible, produced by men who were passive mouthpieces of the voice of God.

Did we call such an attitude piety? We should not have done so. For this is not true piety. It rejects God's way of doing things. Luke's vocabulary and literary style are different from those of Mark. Paul has a style and way of thinking that differ from those of the writer of Hebrews. These are facts. And a fact is a thing to reverence; it must shape our theology. We do not defend or magnify the Bible by denying the human factor in its composition. We rather reject the Bible that exists in favor of one that God did not see fit to give to men. He used human authors; their personal background, their literary style, and their special interests play a plain and noteworthy part in the production of the Bible. We do not reject the canon when we say this. We simply help to make clear what the nature of the canon is. This collection of books shows God's work and revelation in history, and supremely in Christ, but they were written by limited and fallible human beings, who were used to give permanent form to the record and revelation they attested. To accept the canon does not mean to deny the human factor or the literary activity of ancient men.

b. Far removed from those who believe that God dictated the books of the Bible to passive human authors are the people who so stress the human factor that they completely reject the idea of the canon. Yet the two views have much in common. They have a common axiom, usually unexpressed: If God is behind these books, if it is justified to set them apart as a special collection of permanent authority in the Church, then they must not show human differences or give evidence of human workmanship.

In fact, what prevents some people from accepting the concept of the canon is the inescapable fact that these books reflect a very human process of authorship. They show limitations of outlook and understanding. They often deal with the passing situations of little groups. These are human productions, the product of certain small groups and limited individuals of a bygone day. So some would say that to set them apart in a canon and claim for them permanent authority gives them too much importance. In a worthy canon the human, the transient, the fallible, the individual could have no place. It would be the direct dictation of God.

This is the expressed or implied view of many honest critics. And we must agree that they are essentially right about the literary facts. The marks of individual authorship are on almost all these books. Many passages give evidence that the writer has adopted formulas, confessions, and hymns that have taken form in the worship and teaching of the group. Both Testaments reflect the use of oral tradition which has been shaped by continual telling and retelling. The Biblical writers often used written sources, whose authors are unknown to us; this occurs in the Pentateuch, in the historical sections of the Old Testament, in the Synoptic Gospels, and quite likely in Acts. The prophetic books of the Old Testament show marks of editing of the prophetic utterances.

When these writers use their sources they feel free to quote inexactly. In the New Testament, for example, a large portion of the quotations from the Old Testament do not agree exactly with either the Hebrew or the Greek version of the Old Testament. The writers of Matthew and Luke, who used the Gospel of Mark as a source, did not hesitate to substitute their own stylistic habits for some words they found in Mark; even in quoting the words of Jesus they saw no wrong in giving a free report of what had come to them in their source. We would not escape the problem if we were to deny that they used a written source: it would still be true that they do not completely agree in their versions of what Jesus said.

If we turn to the study of how these authors *thought,* we again find differences. Paul does not think as does the writer of The Epistle of James. I would not call James " a right strawy epistle " as Luther did (Luther himself had better things to say about James than this one famous quotation would suggest). Yet it is clear that the author of James did not think in just the way Paul did. James was of different temperament; he faced a different problem; and he used Paul's key words with a somewhat different content. Paul wanted to say how sinners get right with God: he said that it is not by works which earn a good standing, but by the free grace of God, which man gratefully accepts in a faith that is complete trust and commitment to God through Christ. James wanted professing Christians to live up to their position; he said that it was not enough to profess faith; one must also show in his life the evidence of sincere faith in actual Christian living; to use Paul's words, James wanted to see " faith working through love " (Gal. 5:6). We may say that there is no irreconcilable difference between Paul and James; we may say that Paul saw more deeply than James; but we must also say that they have different outlooks and show their human limitations and interests.

This variation between writers comes out perhaps most prominently in the presence of four Gospels in our New

Testament. If we were not so used to it, the fact that the Bible gives four different versions of the life and teaching of Jesus would astonish and puzzle us. It is not to be wondered at that shortly after the middle of the second century Tatian wove the four Gospels into one continuous work. He called it the "Diatessaron," which literally means "through four," and he gave it in Syriac translation to the Eastern churches. It is easy to understand why his Diatessaron proved popular for centuries. It gave a unity to the Gospel story which the four separate Gospels apparently lacked. But there are four Gospels. They reflect the interests of four authors. The human factor appears here as throughout the Bible.

This does not nullify the canon. It is the way God works. Apart from the unique coming of God into human life in Jesus Christ — and even there human limitations were a fact which Jesus himself confessed — God has worked and still works through imperfect human instruments. He did it in the leaders and spokesmen of Biblical times. He did it in the writers of the Biblical books. He does it in the leaders and servants of the Church. And he does it through this collection of books which so obviously bear the marks of human workmanship. It is, of course, a confession of faith that he has worked or does work in these ways, but these four ways all involve the use of individual human agents.

No doubt many Christians secretly or unconsciously believe that when God works through a person he renders that person passive; God simply uses the human hand or tongue as a material tool for the divine action or utterance. That pagan idea is very old. Some Jews shared it. The first century Alexandrian Jew Philo had it. To many, the highest way to let God work is for man to lose thoughtful consciousness, to be inactive, and merely to let God work through the breathing tool of the human body.

There were Christians at Corinth in Paul's day who held a similar idea. They thought that if God seized a person and made him speak with tongues without the use of his rational faculties, this was a greater spiritual gift than prophecy. Paul denied it. He insisted that five words spoken with the understanding were better than ten thousand words uttered in uncontrolled frenzy (I Cor. 14:19). In other words, sober thinking and speaking, in which the faculties of the Christian are working at their highest efficiency, are for Paul the setting for the highest working of the Holy Spirit, particularly because this is the way that brings help to other people. We had better keep away from the uncontrolled and the abnormal when we look for the effective way of God's working in man. He uses limited human beings to do his work and speak his messages, and he has the power and resourcefulness to get his work done and his message expressed through human agents who dedicate their gifts to his service.

As we observe the variety of human expression in the Bible we can understand better the nature of the canon. We hear the voice of many prophets; the psalmists reflect many moods; we possess four Gospels; we have letters from several writers. We find the central issues of life approached from different angles; the writers vary in capacity and interests, and they face individual situations, each of which calls for different treatment. This may seem unfortunate and confusing. But it is life, life as we find it in God's world and even in his Church. We may go into any church we choose, and we will find there leaders and people who vary in background, gifts, and needs. To one person or problem or need certain parts of the Bible speak with maximum power. To another person or problem or need other passages carry a greater message. A person may find that a certain passage now speaks to him with a depth and power it has never shown before.

It is thus theologically justifiable and practically grati-fying that the Bible has this variety and richness in its message and usefulness. Toward the middle of the second century the heretic Marcion rejected the Old Testament and formed a canon by uniting a shortened Luke with ten letters of Paul. The Church rejected this narrow limit of Scripture. It clung to the Old Testament, used all four Gospels, and added Acts and letters by other leaders to the ten letters of Paul which Marcion had used. This provided a canon that was inclusive. It gave the Church a rich, varied, resourceful record of the work and revelation of God — a record which could speak to all sorts and condi-tions of men in various regions and at successive times. There is strength rather than weakness in this combination of writings. To be sure, it makes demands on the historical sense and literary understanding of the Church. It forces the Church to see clearly the human factor. The canon so plainly exhibits this factor that any theory of inerrancy is a strained and misleading way of expressing the rich and continual effectiveness of the Bible. But this variety and human expression, used by the Spirit, can guide Christ's Church in faith and life. It enables the Bible to be the Bible of all people and of the whole Church. It is theologi-cally important, therefore, that the Bible has this multiple witness to the gospel of Christ and to the will of God.

5. *Individual Judgment or Church Decision.* The canon is important to both the Christian individual and the Church at large, and we need to take care that neither as-pect of this contrast takes a role which does not rightly belong to it.

a. According to one view, the extent of the canon is a matter for the individual Christian to decide. At least we hear individual Christians, including scholars, make pronouncements on the question with the implied conviction that they are competent to decide it. If it is a basic tenet of Protestantism that the individual Christian has the complete right of private judgment, this position is defensible. But the extent of the right of private judgment has been greatly overstated in certain Protestant circles. The position contains a truth: the Church does not dictate the beliefs and practices of the individual Christian in a rigid and authoritative way. He has a personal responsibility to face God's claim on his mind and life; he must think and speak, worship and act, as a responsible individual. He cannot let his aunt or mother believe and worship for him; he cannot let his Church do his thinking and make his moral decisions. He must answer to God for the right use of his gifts and opportunities.

But it is inconceivable that a real Christian would think and act without reference to the heritage, wisdom, and joint judgment of the Church. To worship, to think, or to act in splendid isolation would deny the basically social nature of the life in Christ. It would ignore the very nature of the Christian life, which is a life of mutual love and helpfulness. It would deny that the Spirit works in and through the Church. We help one another in our thinking as well as in meeting other human needs. What to do with the Bible which we have received in the Church is an important question. Surely a Christian must begin by recognizing that the Church has given him this Bible, that the Church has a witness to its importance and authority, that millions of Christians accept it as the Word of God in some real sense, and that therefore he as an individual Christian will want to consider this question in the setting of the worship, teaching, and fellowship of the Church.

There is a give-and-take in the thinking of a real Christian, and he will be grateful rather than irked that this is so. If the parts of this Bible have helped other people, if the Church has found that this Bible has preserved and includes the message on which it is grateful to build, if other Christians have found a meaning and fitness in a particular book which, so far at least, means little to me, then I need to know these facts and take them into account. If after doing so I still cannot honestly say that a certain book carries the Christian message to me in any definite way, and so does not seem to me to have an essential place in giving the basic witness to the Christian gospel, I may say so, although I must remember that in the past, passages that had meant nothing to me have come alive in the advancing conditions of my life, and that other passages which have never come alive for me have spoken to other Christians. If, even when I remember this, I still must say that to the best of my Christian judgment it would be better for a book not to be included in the canon, that for me it blurs rather than clarifies the Christian message, I may say so; but it still remains true that I did not create the canon, I did not give it its position in the Church at large, and I cannot by myself change it in any decisive way. The formation, the continuance, and any possible change of the canon are things which go beyond the right of the individual Christian. I may share in rethinking the limits of the canon, but I do not create or change the canon by my personal decision.

b. The recognition of the canon is an act of the Church. It is a confession of the worshiping and witnessing Church that in these books it finds the gospel message presented in its fullness and richness, that these books are the ones that we need in order to hear this witness and its claim in its full range and depth. We have the canon only in the Church. If Christianity were only a concern of many independent believers, there would be no canon.

Did the Church, then, create the canon? Did the decision of the Church give these books permanent authority and canonical standing? We had better think carefully about this question. In recent years the Protestant churches have realized more deeply than they had for many decades the vital role of the Church. Protestant leaders speak with vigorous recognition of this role, and sometimes seem to give to the Church full authority and control in both doctrine and life. This is loose speaking, and it departs from true Protestant thinking.

It is true that the Church existed before the New Testament canon was formed. But when the Church recognized the importance of these writings and their right to serve as a standard and authority in the Church, it recognized that the Church was not the original fact. God's work as attested in the gospel was the original fact, which preceded the rise and formation of the Church. The Church, when it is in spiritual health, knows that it is subject to the gospel and not superior to it. It accepted the canon to express that very fact. It put itself under the judgment and rule of a message which it found in these writings and which it confessed had the right to test the Church. The canon therefore contains in its writings the history, the message, the revelation which is prior to and superior to the Church. We must consider the relation of the canon to the Church's tradition in our final discussion, but we must now make this one point clear: the canon is not in its deepest and truest sense the creation of the Church. In a sense the Church did form the canon, but in so doing it recognized that these writings preceded in content and outrank in authority the developing Church.

If this is so, what authority has the Church to declare the canon permanently closed? Most Protestant Christians undoubtedly consider the canon irrevocably and finally closed. Some would regard as blasphemy any suggestion of a change. But they are not real Protestants when they do so.

The Reformation leaders soon learned, not only from their study of Church history, but also from their dealings with existing Church authorities and councils, that the leaders and councils of the Church can make mistakes. They frankly declared that the decisions of Church leaders have no permanent, binding authority. Sometimes they singled out certain early councils and accepted the confessions and decisions of those councils as authoritative for the Church of their day. But they were clear that it is the Bible and not earlier decisions of Church leaders that has basic authority. Those earlier decisions, even when right, do not become part of Scripture, nor do they become permanent ecclesiastical law binding on all later generations. The Bible is the test of true faith and right thinking.

If we choose to be Protestants, this must remain our position. We certainly must treat with respect and study with care the confessions and council decisions of the Churches, especially those of the ancient and Reformation days. But if we give to the Church, even to our own denomination, the power to define doctrine, including the doctrine of the canon, with a permanently binding and inescapable legal validity, we have adopted in principle the Roman Catholic position, that the Church in the last analysis is supreme even over the Scripture. This we cannot and should not do.

To many earnest Protestants this conclusion will seem to leave the Church in uncertainty and insecurity. In answering this objection, let us ignore for the moment the fact that the canon has not been unanimously fixed in the whole Church at any time since the first century; let us ignore the fact that it is not so fixed today. Let us ask the crucial question: If the canon is not finally fixed, what can we believe in? I suggest God.

It is of the very nature of the Christian life that it can never possess a perfectly clear and objectively demonstrated basis. We walk by faith and not by the decisions of the Reformers and the Westminster fathers. Even if they were right in their view of the canon — and I am ready to accept their decision as the one in which I gladly join as a confessing Christian — we agree with them not because they are the final authority which controls our thought, but by our own confession of the same faith that they confessed in their decisions.

The canon is a theological issue. The doctrine of the canon, like all doctrines, is a matter not for objective proof but for grateful confession. As we gladly hear these books read in the worship of the Church, as we receptively study and hear the teaching of these books in the Church, as we gratefully use these writings and find that by the work of God's Spirit they speak the gospel and bring God and his will to us and to our Church, as we find that precisely these writings preserve the heritage of the Church, and as we find that they express in rich faithfulness the gospel on which the Church and our own Christian faith is founded, the canon becomes real to us. If we thus confess as a Church and as members of the Church that this is our Bible, then we have the canon.

We really have no canon on any basis except this Church-fostered, faith-founded, grateful contemporary witness. And we will have no canon tomorrow except by the renewal of that confession and witness. But we may have it every day on that basis, and we may believe that the Bible will go on proving itself to be canonical as God speaks to us through its words and claims our lives by its message.

III

Is the Old Testament Christian Scripture?

OUR Old Testament was the Bible of Jesus and the apostles. They accepted and used it as Scripture; it contained for them authoritative divine revelation. Thus the Church had a Bible from the beginning. Our Old Testament was the sole Scripture of the Church for the first few generations. The first Christians did not ask whether they should have a Scripture or whether this was the Scripture they should accept. As Jews they already had our Old Testament, and without raising any question they kept it.

How had this Old Testament become canonical for the Jews? What did it contain? We can here trace the growth of the Old Testament canon only in broad outline, for our interest is in the place that the Old Testament held in the first century and in the later Church. We postpone the question of the Jewish attitude toward the Old Testament Apocrypha. It is a large question which has been much discussed in past centuries of Church history, and it is now a particularly vital issue. Therefore we give it separate study in the next chapter.

The Old Testament books were written during a period which extended over the greater part of a thousand years. Their collection into definite groups and their winning of

43

canonical position was a process that took several centuries. It is not our task to study the process by which early oral traditions and written sources finally found their place in the completed books. We want to know how and when these completed books were combined to form the Old Testament canon.

THE FORMATION OF THE HEBREW CANON

The germ of the idea of the canon was no doubt earlier than Israel clearly realized. The laws of their common life were traced back to God. The unique series of rugged prophetic figures claimed to speak the very word of the Lord. The worship of Israel was held to be prescribed by God. So the conviction could arise that writings which contained such materials were authoritative and normative. But we cannot reconstruct the process by which that conviction took form. We must look at the essential results.

THE LAW

The first important thing to note is that the Old Testament canon took form in three great divisions: the Torah or Law, the Prophets, and the Writings. It is not possible to state with certainty the exact date at which the Pentateuch, consisting of the five books ascribed to Moses, was completed. A date in the middle of the fifth century B.C. is at least fairly close to the truth. Almost at once, and certainly before 400 B.C., these books were considered authoritative or canonical. Thus the Law became the first part of the canon to attain such recognition. Among the Jews it has never lost its place of priority. They have always considered the Law the Scripture par excellence. This attitude has not been carried over into the Christian view. But we can never understand Judaism if we forget how unique a role the Law plays in Jewish life.

THE PROPHETS

Not long after the middle of the third century B.C., and certainly not later than about 200 B.C., the formation of the collection of prophetic books was completed, and they were soon recognized as authoritative for the Jews. The author of the Apocryphal work Ecclesiasticus, writing early in the second century B.C., knows the Prophets as a completed collection.

It is important to note what books this prophetic collection contained. It included the books of Joshua, Judges, Samuel, and Kings; the larger prophetic books of Isaiah, Jeremiah, and Ezekiel; and the twelve shorter prophetic books, which were united in one group and treated as a unit. In a famous passage, Jeshua (in Greek, Jesus) the son of Sirach, the writer of Ecclesiasticus, says: " Let us now praise famous men " (ch. 44:1), and he then passes in review the great figures of Israel's history. The names he gives and the order in which he mentions these figures show that he knew the prophetic books as a definite collection; he also mentions " the twelve prophets " as a special group within this larger collection (ch. 49:10).

In later Jewish theory we find the view that all the Prophets, and indeed all the Old Testament writings, date between the time of Moses and the reign of the Persian ruler Artaxerxes I (465-424 B.C.). This period was regarded as the time of inspiration and prophecy. Not every prophetic book actually dates early enough to fit that theory, but sometime before 200 B.C. they all existed in final form and stood united in the definite collection of recognized authority.

THE WRITINGS

The third part of the Hebrew canon, the Writings, had
no unity of content or literary type, nor did it find such
ready acceptance as did the Law and the Prophets. But that
this third part of the canon existed as a separate collection,
at least in nucleus, is clear from two references to it by the
grandson of Jeshua the son of Sirach. About 132 B.C. he
translated his grandfather's Ecclesiasticus into Greek. To
the translation he prefixed a preface. In it he once refers
to the Scripture as " the Law and the Prophets and the
other books of our fathers," and another reference speaks
of " the Law and the Prophets and the rest of the books."
But the grandson does not specify how many writings and
just which ones this third collection contained in his day.

Our Gospels give a little help on this question. They
report sayings of Jesus which seem to imply that the third
part of the Old Testament canon existed in his day (Matt.
23:35; Luke 24:44). Josephus, the Jewish historian, reports
at the end of the first century, as a fact of long standing, a
canon which in all probability was precisely the Hebrew
canon we now know. But there is still a trace of uncertainty
in even these witnesses. The more explicit Talmudic passage in Baba Bathra 14b–15a rests on early tradition, but
was not written down until after A.D. 200. The accepted
Jewish canon of Jesus' day apparently was that which we
know, but we cannot be certain that a definite decision
had been made.

WHEN WAS THE HEBREW CANON COMPLETED?

The question as to when the Hebrew canon was completed is important. But it is difficult to give a conclusive
answer, because of the evidence that in the first century
A.D. the Jews still carried on spirited debate as to the right

of certain books to be included in their canon. We hear echoes of disputes especially concerning Esther, Proverbs, Ecclesiastes, the Song of Songs, and Ezekiel. It will be noticed that all but one of these disputed books were among those finally included in the part of the Jewish canon called the Writings. This is a reminder that the Writings constituted the last part of that canon to attain clear acceptance as canonical.

It must be remembered that the debates on these points occurred in rabbinical circles. They represent the Pharisaic tradition of Jesus' day. We have no proof that the Sadducees ever accepted these Writings as Scripture. The discoveries of manuscript fragments at *Qumrân* indicate that among the Essenes a number of the Writings, while known and used, may not have been accepted as fully canonical. This conclusion, though by no means certain, has been suggested because some *Qumrân* manuscripts of the Writings are written on inferior material and in a less formal script than we find in the usual manuscripts of canonical writings. But the general situation in Palestine and specifically in the synagogues was that which the rabbinical leaders represent. Their debates are of central interest.

Did these first century debates, which persisted over a number of generations, precede a basic agreement to accept these books as canonical? Or did they follow such a decision, so that they were in fact an echo of the issues debated when the decision was first made? We can make no absolutely certain choice between these alternatives. A trace of uncertainty lingers on, as though to remind the Christian that his final certainty is not in a book but in God.

But while absolute certainty is not attainable, it is probable, as a considerable number of scholars hold, that the basic decision as to the canonical list of the Writings had

been made before the ministry of Jesus. A more official
settlement of the issue appears to have followed about
A.D. 90, at the Jewish council at Jamnia, a city on the
coastal plain of Palestine. That the first century debates
were reactions against a generally recognized previous decision of Jewish leaders would seem to be indicated by the
fact that Ezekiel was one of the disputed books. Without
doubt this book had long had canonical standing. If, then,
it was still subject to challenge, some of the Writings were
likewise open to reconsideration, and could perhaps be
more easily challenged because their canonical position was
on the whole less secure and more recently granted.

   The arrangement of books in the Septuagint may suggest that by the first century A.D. the Writings had already
obtained general recognition as canonical. We possess only
Christian copies of this Greek translation of the Old Testament, but if the first century Greek-speaking Jews used
the Septuagint in the form that the ancient Christians have
handed down to us, they mingled the books of the Prophets
with those of the Writings. They did not keep clear the
three divisions of the Hebrew canon. This suggests that
the Writings were regarded as on the same level with the
Prophets, which were generally recognized by Jews as canonical. While, therefore, some doubts and disputes lingered on, we may say that the Hebrew Old Testament
canon was rather well fixed by the time of Jesus. It must
be remembered, however, that from the Jewish point of
view the Law had a prominence and authority which did
not attach to the other books. It must also be remembered,
as we shall note again in the next chapter, that the Septuagint as we know it contains more books than does the
Hebrew canon. But one thing seems clear: the makers of
the Septuagint valued the Writings as highly as they did
the Prophets.

Even the formal decision of A.D. 90 at Jamnia did not stop discussion. Objection to individual books occurs occasionally in later times, not only among rabbinical utterances, but also in Christian writers. The Book of Esther is a prominent example. The Talmud contains an echo of later Jewish debate about this book. The Christian Melito of Sardis made a special journey to Palestine to learn the number and order of books that should be included in the Old Testament; in his report he omitted Esther. So did Athanasius in his famous Easter Letter of A.D. 367. The reasons are not given, but the lack of reference to God and the narrow, vengeful spirit may have troubled some readers. One Jewish criticism apparently was that this book established a new feast which was not prescribed in the Pentateuch. But this feast was established, and the use of The Book of Esther at this feast seems to have been a fixed practice in Palestine, before the days of Jesus. So the canonical rank of The Book of Esther was probably widely recognized before the first century.

Why Christians Accept the Old Testament

But why do we as Christians accept this Jewish canon? What is the basic theological ground on which our decision is based? We do not accept that canon simply because these books, as far as we can determine, were canonical to the Jews of Palestine in the days of Jesus and the apostles. That, of course, is a notable fact. But the Church cannot accept so crucial a decision on the authority of a non-Christian group. The basic reasons must come from within the Christian Church.

A far stronger reason is that Jesus and the apostles unhesitatingly accepted the Old Testament as their Scripture. We accept Jesus Christ as Master and Lord, and we regard the apostles as trustworthy witnesses to the gospel. It would

be difficult for us to reject the very writings that they accepted and used as their Bible. Moreover, if we accept the
New Testament writings as normative, it would be hard
to justify the discarding of the Old Testament, for to all
the New Testament writers the Old Testament was
Scripture.

The case in favor of the Old Testament becomes stronger
when we recall the repeated decisions of Church councils
which have always included these Old Testament writings
in the canon. Their decisions do not completely close the
issue, but it would be hard to defend a drastic departure
from the view of Jesus and the apostles when their position
has been accepted by the Christian conviction of nineteen
centuries.

In the last analysis, however, the decision to keep the
Old Testament cannot be made for us by other generations. The final question is whether the Old Testament is
Scripture to us in the Church today. And this question
each generation must answer for itself. Its answer is a
confession, a decision of faith. Each Christian generation
must say for itself whether it finds in the Old Testament
the work and revelation of God. It must say whether it
finds here an essential message which still speaks with authority and power, so that we must include this Old Testament in our canon and use it as Scripture in our Church.
This decision, this reaffirmation of the inherited Christian
position, the Church is continually making, and I gratefully share in this continued acceptance of the Old Testament as Scripture.

WHY WE MUST KEEP THE OLD TESTAMENT

Let us look at the advantages and the necessity of keeping the Old Testament as part of Christian Scripture. We
need not pause long over the literary genius and lofty

thinking of many of these writings. They rank high in these respects, but that would not make them Scripture with canonical authority. Nor is it enough, though it is a great thing and almost unique in the ancient world, that the prevailing tone of their thinking reflects a pure and reverent monotheism. This fact goes far to explain how Judaism won proselytes in the days just before and during the New Testament period. But it alone would not warrant making the Old Testament a permanent part of Christian Scripture. Neither does the generally high moral quality of the Old Testament teaching constitute the basic reason for giving canonical status to this collection. It was not as a general ethical code that the Old Testament became Scripture for the Church.

A more specific service of the Old Testament is that it gives us the essential background of the New Testament revelation and writings. No one will ever rightly understand the gospel who does not have clearly in mind the Old Testament preparation for it. The Old Testament had not finished its service when it had prepared the way for Christ and the Church. The Church continuously needs the Old Testament to understand fully what it has in its Christian faith. This fact is suggested by the plain evidence of the New Testament. Its writers use the Old Testament and they witness to its essential place in New Testament thinking. To use and understand the New Testament, one needs also to use the Old Testament and grow in understanding of it.

To the Christian, the Old Testament is vitally related to Christ and the specifically Christian revelation. Its story is an integral part of the one purposeful and redemptive working of God which finds its climax in Christ and its outworking in the Church. The Old Testament thus attests the basic Christian viewpoint that history is the scene

and the means of the specific redemptive working of God.
It records and interprets an essential segment of that story
on which all later Christian faith and thought is based.
And it points on to the central figure and events of that
story.

The Old Testament thus reveals God's working and
purpose in history, and it promises God's full revelation
and redemptive action in Christ. But it is not outworn
when Christ has come and done his work; its history and
teaching keep pointing to him. The Church really sees and
grasps God's intent and saving method only as it keeps
continually in view the full sweep of the Biblical story,
of which the Old Testament tells so important a part.
Moreover, because the later conditions of God's people in
Christ often parallel the Old Testament situations of God's
people Israel, the Old Testament, rightly used, supple-
ments the New Testament as a guide for Christian worship
and life, and so proves fruitful as a continuing Word of
God for Christian people. All this implies a real unity in
the Bible, a unity that grows out of the unity of the purpose and action of God.

Wrong Uses of the Old Testament

It should be honestly recognized, however, that real
dangers threaten when the Church uses the Old Testament as Scripture. Only if we face these dangers frankly
can we use with Christian wisdom this part of Christian
Scripture. What are the problems to keep in mind?

One problem arises from the sheer bulk of the Old
Testament. This in itself is no evil, nor is it necessarily a
dangerous thing. Nevertheless, since the Old Testament
occupies three fourths of the Bible, the careless Christian
may unconsciously permit this larger portion of Scripture
to dominate Christian thinking. This would obscure the

central and normative role of Christ.

Another difficulty in the Christian use of the Old Testament is that it gives no direct witness to Jesus Christ. This could lead Christians to ignore the vital relation of the Old Testament story to Christ. Such a mistake would be highly damaging for the Church. If it should lead Christians to take the Old Testament as basic, and to regard Christ as only a supplementary addition to the main portion and message of Scripture, it would be a fatal influence. If, on the other hand, it should lead the Church to ignore the pre-Christian history of Israel and to strive desperately by allegory and highly developed typology to find only Christ in every Old Testament word, it would be a warping and misleading thing. The absence of direct and specific reference to Jesus must be recognized, but the Old Testament story must be accepted as real history and must be related to the story of Jesus and the Church.

A further problem in the Old Testament is found in its passages of definitely sub-Christian character. We may recall the attempt of Martin Luther to justify the bigamy of his prince by reference to the Old Testament practice of polygamy. There are passages of unforgiving spirit, as when Israel or its king is reminded of its enemies' actions and told, " You shall not forget " (Deut. 7:2; 23:3-6; 25:17-19) . Something less than the highest standards appears in The Book of Esther. It reflects a good sense of the place of Israel in God's plan, but its militant nationalism and wholesale bloodshed are open to definite criticism. We have no right to cover these flaws by allegory, nor should we make tortuous attempts to show that these people really lived in full loyalty to Christian standards. They often failed to do so. Upon occasion they failed to grasp and teach the full will of God. The Old Testament repeatedly indicates the wrongful character of such actions and teaching. But even where it does not, we must not try to justify what was less than God's true will.

Another problem is present in the nationalistic and exclusive ring of much Old Testament expression. There are noble passages which rise above this limited outlook, but they do not dominate the history. We may say that Israel, by concentration upon its worship and service of God, and by stubborn separation from the idolatry and low moral standards of the surrounding pagan world, did what it had to do to keep from compromising the faith it had been given to preserve and defend. There is much truth in this view, but it is not the whole truth. Israel and its leaders frequently showed a narrow spirit which fostered pride in their own privilege and fed contempt for those whom God had not so favored. We find traces of selfishness where there could have been a sense of sympathy and mission. This nationalistic, exclusive, and selfish note does not belong in the gospel.

One other danger rises from the prominence of the legal and priestly features of the Old Testament. We have already noted that in the formation of the Old Testament canon the Law, with its ritual and sacrifices and priestly ministry, took and maintained a higher rank than the Prophets and the Writings. It is only right to point out that the Pentateuch contains much besides legal regulations and sacrificial prescriptions. There is immensely important history of God's dealings with his people. There is prophetic power. But the laws and the ritual also are there. They are present in that part of Scripture to which the Jews attached supreme importance. They put their stamp on Judaism and on rabbinical thought. And whenever the Christian Church has let the legal and priestly regulations of the Pentateuch gain a shaping influence on the worship and life of the Church and its members, a sub-Christian spirit has taken hold of the Church. Such a result is not necessary; it is not right; but it is always possible with the Old Testament in the canon, and it has happened often in the life of the Church.

These drawbacks and potential dangers are real. They have led some to try to sever the connection of Christianity with the Old Testament. Marcion in the second century was of this mind. He discarded the Old Testament entirely; he replaced it by another Scripture, which combined a shortened Gospel of Luke and ten letters of Paul, so edited as to remove most traces of the deep kinship of the Christian message with the Old Testament. The twentieth century scholar Adolf von Harnack, who had an obvious admiration for Marcion, conceded that when Christianity appeared and the New Testament was written the Church could only keep the Old Testament; but he thought it a fateful thing that circumstances forced the Reformation to do likewise, and he was convinced that to keep the purity of Christian faith the Church must now deny that the Old Testament is Scripture. He thought it tragic for the Church to cling to so outworn and misleading a book. Few scholars — apart from the partisan Nazi propagandists against the Jews and their Scripture — have spoken with so sweeping a rejection of the Old Testament. But others have felt keenly the differences between the two Testaments, and occasionally one justifies the keeping of the Old Testament by using it only to bring out the contrast between its low spiritual and moral level and the higher plane of the New Testament.

The sound thinking of the Church has refused to accept this extreme position. To reject the Old Testament would be to discredit the New Testament, the apostolic witness, and even the message of Jesus himself. It is hard to see how one can share the Christian faith without accepting

the Old Testament as an integral and permanent part of
the Christian Scripture. Our question is how we can properly recognize the limitations of the Old Testament and
guard against the damage that wrong use of it could do
to the Church. How are we to understand the Old Testament so that it takes its true place as an integral part of
Christian Scripture?

THE OLD TESTAMENT WITNESS TO CHRIST

We can do this only by keeping clearly in mind the basis
on which Jesus and the apostles accepted the Old Testament. It is the basis that the Church affirmed when it kept
the Old Testament in the canon. Though the fact is sometimes ignored, it is as clear as any historical fact can be that
Jesus and his followers accepted the Old Testament because of its link with him and his work, and because it was
in a real sense a witness to him. The Church saw that the
Old Testament was a Christ-related book, and so kept it
as Christian Scripture.

This is the test. Unless the Old Testament witnesses to a
divine work and revelation that is indissolubly linked to
that which we see in Christ, unless it points to Christ and
witnesses to Christ, it has no place in the Christian Bible.
And unless it is interpreted in the light of God's work in
Christ, so that the entire Bible is a Christ-centered Bible,
it is not accepted in a Christian sense. How shall we understand the Old Testament so as to preserve and protect this
unified, Christ-centered character of the Bible?

This Old Testament story is the historical preparation
and background for Jesus and the first Christians. But
this is not all. Every succeeding Christian generation must
know and use this Testament in order to see in true per-
spective the divine work and revelation in Christ. Thus
while it portrays preparation and background, it is not

a mere temporary scaffolding. It still has an essential role in presenting to the Church the word of God concerning his will and our duty. When we want to learn what God has done that is of basic importance for all generations of our Church, what he has revealed himself to be, what he wants of men, and what his purpose is, we must take the Old Testament into account as well as the New. The Old Testament is not yet the story of the coming and redemptive work of Jesus Christ. We must let it stand as preparation and promise. We must not read the whole story of Christian salvation back into it. But it tells its part of the total story on which our faith and hope are based.

This honored position of the Old Testament does not mean that we put everything in both Testaments on one level. There is a continuity in what God did in the total period that they cover. There is a basic agreement in their picture of the purpose and work of God. They show a deep unity within which we find manifold variety and human differences. They offer us a rich heritage of permanently authoritative revelation which speaks to the Church with urgency and power. But the center is in Christ.

The Old Testament is not consistently on the level of what Christ was and did. It has to be used in the light of Christ and with the limitation and control that God's work in Christ gives us. The practice of using all parts of Scripture as equally binding, without reference to the center in Christ, is a fatal return to a lawbook conception of revelation. It ignores the fact that there is a history of salvation, that in this history God works out his purpose, and that his purpose and his revelation are not so clear in the early stages as they are in Jesus Christ and in the Spirit's witness to him in the Apostolic Church. Unless we make Christ central, unless we give the New Testament's specific witness to Christ the decisive role in the Bible, we permit the very bulk of the Old Testament to hold the Church at a sub-Christian or pre-Christian level.

METHODS OF INTERPRETATION

By what method of interpretation can we properly show the relation of the Old Testament to Christ and the New Testament?

1. *The Search for Allegory*. The tie cannot be found in allegory, that is, by finding in every event and person and name and rule of the Old Testament a hidden reference to Christ or to some aspect of the New Testament gospel. It was a sound instinct that led the authors of the Westminster Confession of Faith to insist that " the true and full sense of Scripture . . . is not manifold but one," namely, the historical and literal sense which the passage had when it was written. The persistent attempt to find two or three or four senses in a passage of Scripture buries the historical meaning under a flood of subjective fancy and speculation. It is not exegesis but eisegesis. It would be even worse to deny, as the second century Epistle of Barnabas was inclined to do, that the Old Testament had a historical and literal meaning. This would imply that the only meaning of the Old Testament was its allegorical reference to Christ and the Christian gospel.

Such interpretation would be false. God actually dealt with real people, and what happened and what was said related directly to their situation. God did not ignore the Old Testament people's needs and speak solely of the still-future New Testament history. He dealt with the people who were then living; he spoke to them. It later proved true that in a legitimate sense his dealings and word possessed a continuing meaning and authority. But this insight must never obscure the basic historical and literal meaning of the original account; it must not be developed in the form of a systematic allegory of the Old Testament material.

The reality of God's working in history at each successive stage is the basic fact to recognize. The historical meaning is the real meaning of each passage.

It should be added that the literal meaning includes poetic imagery, figures of speech, and even a double meaning, wherever the original writer himself intended such a poetic, figurative, or double meaning. The insistence on the literal sense says that we must let the passage mean what the writer intended it to mean. If his words later, when joined with other writings, can support a richer message, if when seen in the light of later events they can be fitted into a larger pattern to give a deeper grasp of God's revelation in history, we must gladly recognize the fact. But no later or wider use of the material must ever obscure the fact that the writer spoke to his own time. No later use can be allowed to cancel or ignore the intended meaning of the original author. The later use must grow out of and make honest use of his meaning.

Perhaps our greatest question concerning allegory rises from the presence of the Song of Songs in the canon. It was long considered to be an allegory of the love of God for Israel or the Church or the believer. But it really is poetic portrayal of human love. As Paul's use of the marriage relation suggests (Eph. 5:32), the language of human love can express in a secondary way the relation between God and his people. But as the experience of Israel with the Baal fertility cults showed only too well, there are dangers in this use of language for religious worship and thought, and such use must be kept within strict limits.

It is worth noting that though there are allegorical passages in the New Testament, the number is very few, particularly when compared with such writers as the first century Hellenistic Jew Philo, whose works are a maze of allegorical interpretations. Allegory was a common and widely accepted method of argument in the first century. But the New Testament use of the Old Testament is not basically allegorical. In a few passages the gospel is illustrated by allegory, but it is never grounded on it or dependent on it. The basis of the gospel is the historical action of God in Israel and through Christ.

2. *The Use of Typology*. More legitimate, and more frequent in the New Testament, is the typological use of the Old Testament. Here some Old Testament person or event is seen to embody a truth or a working of God similar to that found in the New Testament. In the earlier stage the working of God appears in a preparatory form and in a lesser way; once the fulfillment has come the parallel and similarity can be seen and appreciated.

This typology contains a real truth. There is a deep unity in the work and revelation of God in the two Testaments. So naturally there is similarity between his earlier and later ways of working; there is consistency in the way he wills and works and reveals himself in the two periods. Since he has a consistent purpose and works toward his chosen goal, his earlier work will hint at and point toward the climactic achievement of his aim. It is natural and inevitable that the Christian now sees in the Old Testament earlier expressions of what finds fuller and more central expression in the work of Jesus Christ. The kindly work of the good shepherds whom Israel knew points forward to the Good Shepherd, Christ. The way Moses and David faithfully led Israel points forward to the way Jesus led his followers. And even when, as is usually the case, the New Testament gives a deeper meaning to the Old Testament words, we may recognize a certain fitness in the parallel. This happens, for example, when the pledge of the Promised Land is later understood to mean the gift of salvation and blessing in a more than material sense.

But it must be frankly stated that typology, though found in many passages, holds a minor role in the New Testament. This is good, for typology has great limitations. In the first place, it may draw attention away from the literal historical meaning of the Old Testament. Rightly used, it lets the historical meaning stand forth clearly, as allegory fails to do. But it still may tend to find the main significance of the Old Testament event in its similarity to the New Testament parallel rather than in any real work of God in the Old Testament situation. A sound exegesis and application of the Old Testament will stay steadfastly with the historical meaning; it will not let itself warp or obscure that meaning to provide a neat similarity to a New Testament event. It will never let the attention turn entirely to the New Testament event. It will build upon the original, literal meaning.

In the second place, typology does not give the original and obvious meaning of the Old Testament passage. Such a parallel becomes clear only after the New Testament event. We must not imagine that it was obvious to the Old Testament writer or to the original readers of his work.

In the third place, not every passage carries a typological meaning. In most Old Testament passages it is strained and therefore wrong to try to find such a meaning. Even where the parallel and similarity seem clear to the Christian consciousness, such an interpretation is almost always selective; some aspects of the Old Testament event, person, or saying are not parallel or similar to the New Testament item, and these dissimilarities have to be ignored to develop the typology.

If we are quite frank about it, this selectivity means that the Old Testament passage itself does not carry the typology. Later Christian thought sees that in certain striking respects some Old Testament passages offer parallels to New Testament figures and events. It ignores the differences and points out the parallels, to show that the working of God has an essential consistency and moves forward to the clearer and more central and decisive outworking of God's purpose. This can be a helpful way of showing this unity of God's working and the unity of the Scriptures, but it also reminds us of the variety in form and expression. It is a caution not to take typology as the basic tool of Old Testament interpretation.

This is especially advisable when we remember that our Christian typology often reinterprets the Old Testament passage, so that the material event or promise of the Old Testament is used as a parallel to a spiritual gift or blessing or relation in the New. This unconscious shift in meaning as we move from the Old Testament to the New Testament parallel really means that this typology is a helpful application rather than a strict exegesis of the Old Testament. It uses the passage in the light of Christ and the central gospel, but it goes beyond the mind and intent of the Old Testament writer.

3. *A Book of Prophecy*. The New Testament also interprets the Old Testament as a book of prophecy. It finds this forward-looking, predictive element not only in the sayings of the prophets, but throughout the entire Old Testament. Moses is a prophet (Deut. 18:15, 18), and passages of the Pentateuch are found to be prophetic in character. Statements of the so-called historical books as well as of The Psalms and other poetic and Wisdom books are likewise cited as prophecy.

There is deep truth in this view that the entire Old Testament looks forward to the central action of God for his people. The Biblical view of life is not static. God does

not deal with his people in detached episodes. He has an
ongoing plan and his people have an ongoing life. The
spokesman of God must speak of what God has done, and
he must be vividly aware of the fact that the living God
is at work in the present; but he must also see the incomplete nature of what has thus far been done. He must look
forward in faith and hope to the fuller realization of the
divine purpose. Particularly in the later books of the Old
Testament this note of expectation and prediction may be
felt. It is a witness to the fact that the Old Testament by
itself can never be an adequate Scripture; it alone cannot
permanently satisfy the needs of God's people for a witness to the revelation of their God.

Yet to regard the Old Testament as a book of prophecy
is no adequate view of its relation to Christ and the
Church. In the first place, by far the vast majority of the
Old Testament verses cannot be forced to yield a specific
prophecy of any Christian event or person.

In the second place, the fact that the original intent of
the Old Testament writer was to speak to his own day must
not be lost from view. We cannot ignore this literal historical meaning, and we dare not launch out on a program
of finding double meanings in each Scripture passage.

In the third place, we must look deeper than mechanical
correspondence between an Old Testament passage and a
New Testament event. In Matt. 21:2-7 an Old Testament
poetic passage, which in poetic parallelism uses two different phrases to refer in parallel lines to the same animal,
is used to suggest that Jesus rode into Jerusalem on two
animals. This is a devotional and homiletic practice which
does not really further historical or theological understanding.

Finally, since the Biblical story reveals an advance in
the working of God, so that a purer and fuller and truer

expression of his purpose emerges in his later central action in Christ, we do not expect to hear the Old Testament express the gospel facts with such clarity as the New Testament does. There is a type of prophetic proof which in effect puts all this Biblical history on one level. It finds gospel events as clearly and specifically predicted in the Old Testament as they are fulfilled in the New. This ignores the ongoing work of God in history and assigns to the prediction a clarity which it does not inherently have.

The forward look is real, but it is not so explicit as is often thought. When I read Isa., ch. 53, for example, I am convinced that this writer, led by the Spirit of God, reaches out to just the kind of leader and redeemer who came in Jesus Christ. But I am also convinced that he had no such clear picture of the historical Jesus as modern newspaper photographers and reporters could have combined to give, had they covered Jesus' trial and crucifixion. It is enough — and it is a rich gift — that this great Old Testament writer was led by the divine Spirit to sketch in such vivid outline his anticipation of the sacrificial, vicarious, redemptive suffering of Jesus Christ. He did not know who it was that would perfectly embody that character. He may have had in mind partly his people but more definitely one of the leaders of his people. As far as he thought of an individual, he may have used traits of one who had already appeared, but his focus was on one who was still to appear. We may say with honesty and truth that what he thus saw found its central and climactic realization in Jesus Christ and his death on the cross, but we need not say and should not say that the Old Testament writer clearly saw Jesus himself.

To me, then, the prophetic strain in the Old Testament is real and significant. It does much to bind the two Testaments together. But it does not appear in most passages;

it must not obscure the immediate historical reference of the writer; it must not be developed in a mechanical manner; it does not give explicit predictions of New Testament persons and events in the clear way in which later Christian thought may rightly connect the two; and it must not take our eye from the central fact, that the Old Testament in its total meaning is a forward-looking book and promises a fuller and decisive action of God.

4. *A Book of Promise.* It may be that we do wrong to use the word " prophecy " so much. It suggests that the Old Testament writer consciously and specifically looked forward to and clearly saw the concrete New Testament events. We may do better to use the word " promise." For there is given to men of faith in the Old Testament a promise and assurance that God will prove faithful; he will carry forward his work; he will achieve his purpose; he will raise up the adequate leader and helper; he will give complete salvation and blessing; he will come to his people in power and love, and he will deliver them and keep them with himself.

The Old Testament is a book of promise to men of faith. It contains promises which find fulfillment in the New Testament, but the fulfillment purifies, deepens, and surpasses the promise, and this transformation of the promise in the act of fulfillment is part of the reason that the mechanical idea of prediction and fulfillment is not adequate to express what God gives in Christ and the gospel.

5. *A Book of Law.* One of the most widely used views of the relation between the two Testaments holds that the Old Testament gives the law and the New Testament gives the gospel. The Old Testament law makes clear the holiness of God and his rightful claim to obedience from men. It thus makes clear the fact of man's sin and the desperate dilemma of disobedient man. Then the New Testament

gives the answer to bankrupt man: the gospel offers him salvation.

There is some truth in this, but it is mixed with much that is misleading. If we look at the Old Testament through the eyes of the Jews, we may set the Law in the center of the picture. We have noted that for them the Law was Scripture to a degree and with an authority which the rest of the Old Testament did not match. We may also note that in the Pharisaism of the first century, and in the rabbinical and Talmudic tradition which Judaism developed, the legal note is prominent. Even in the Christian or any other view, there is in the Old Testament a considerable regulation of life by rules. Its " Church year," its sacrificial and ritual system, its regulation of numerous social situations, its prescription of penalties for violation of the law come readily to mind.

Yet to describe the Old Testament as simply the law is quite wrong. The law is set in a history which is clearly explained to be under God's control. So extensive a history, clearly interpreted in the light of the will of God, must be important from the Old Testament point of view. This history is the scene of God's action and revelation. Moreover, it is given a prophetic interpretation. It is all measured by the prophetic insight that God gave to his spokesmen. Rather than call the Old Testament the law, it would be nearer the truth to call it all prophecy, not in the sense of specific predictions of coming events, but in the sense of a penetrating interpretation which sees the history of God's people under the divine judgment and goodness. We need not overstress this prophetic feature, but it is prominent and pervasive. Furthermore, to call the Old Testament the law is to ignore the element of promise to which we have referred.

Finally, and most important, the aspects of undeserved

divine election, grace, and redemption are so obvious and so persistent that to call the Old Testament the law is but a caricature of the true situation. It is the God who has redeemed Israel from Egypt who gives them the Commandments (Ex. 20:1, 2) . Thus it is the God of grace who claims obedience. The Old Testament is a book that contains the moral demand of God, but it also contains his revelation of his goodness and grace; it speaks of both demand and grace.

It may be noted also that the New Testament makes the same comprehensive demand for total obedience to God's will; it too contains both grace and a moral demand. It is correct to say that in the Old Testament the legal element takes a formal prominence and receives a code development which the New Testament does not parallel, and it is justifiable to say that the gospel stands out in the New Testament with a clarity and fullness that the Old Testament does not equal. But the contrast must not be overdone. The deep and essential unity between the two Testaments, both of which include the demand of God and the grace of God, is the central fact to hold fast.

6. *God's Action in History.* We therefore view the Old Testament as the witness to God's work and revelation in a special history, a history that moved toward and found fulfillment in Jesus Christ and the Apostolic Church of the Spirit.

In this history many great men took their part, but this is not a series of biographies of great men. They were great in so far as God used them and made them great, and their greatness is thus a witness to God's greatness and goodness in his dealings with them.

In this history we find many great teachings, and we can see God at work to bring these people to clearer understanding of his will. But we must not take the Old Testa-

ment or the entire Bible as merely a stage for the steady
growth of great religious ideas. There was much such
growth, but there were also great ideas that came early to
classic expression. Besides, the real interest was not in the
competent thinking of men, for the men were convinced
that they received their great insights through God's working in them.

The interest centered rather in the total working of
God, in which each significant person had a part that fitted
him into the total history. God works and reveals himself
in the history, and it is the history not merely of human
leaders and ideas but mainly of divine action and revelation. It is a real history, which brings positive gifts and
blessings to men of faith as well as definite judgment and
penalty to disobedient members of God's people. It is an
unfinished history, a history that calls for just that continu-
ation which the New Testament gospel offers. This gospel
does not ignore or cancel the message of God's holiness
and moral demand on men, but it offers the redemption
and fellowship and power which restore man to life with
God and to responsible newness of life before God.

Special Ministries of the Old Testament in the Church

The Old Testament is thus a permanent witness to God
as the Creator, the rightful Lord, the authorized Judge, and
the one true Redeemer of his people. These are all aspects
that must be preserved and given their recognition in any
full gospel of the Church. They are features that find their
full witness only when the Old Testament is included in
the Scripture.

This Old Testament is also a permanently helpful guide
to worship, to life insights, and to understanding of the
majestic sweep of the setting of life under God. It is not by

itself adequate for this purpose. But the worshiping and thinking Church finds in the Old Testament abundant resources to aid in the voicing of worship, the probing of God's ways with men, and the sensing of his transcendent majesty and surpassing greatness. In many aspects these resources are not fully paralleled in the New Testament.

This Old Testament, furthermore, gives to all later Christian generations rich resources to help them find what, under Christ, they should do in many of the organized aspects of human life. The small New Testament Church, living under a totalitarian empire and not yet so developed that the social relations of the Church and the Christian were fully developed, did not face all the typical situations of community life which have confronted later Christians. In the Old Testament the people of God know both slavery and freedom; they suffer tyranny at home and from foreign conquerors; they face problems as to how God's people should react under human rulers and in situations of social injustice. There is a reach and variety about these Old Testament situations that the New Testament does not match.

No Christian should study these Old Testament situations without reference to the central message of salvation through Christ. Reference to such situations can help us only when we let the gospel free us from the distorting influence of the legalism and nationalism and exclusivistic selfishness that could result from the use of isolated Old Testament passages. As Christians we face our social situations in the setting of our faith in Christ and our primary social bond in the Church. But it is providential that the Old Testament offers this rich background and supplementary light on the issues of faith, worship, and Christian living.

The Old Testament the Church's Book

In what we have been saying we have assumed that in its final meaning the Old Testament is a Christian book. We do not mean that it must be read as a direct and specific account of the events and teachings of Jesus Christ. Nor do we mean that it is an up-to-date rule book on Christian living. But we do mean that the true way to understand it and the right way to find its proper setting is to link it with the New Testament and interpret it in its unity with Christ and the Church.

This is not the only view that is current today. There are those who consider that the Jews and the Christians have equal rights to the possession of the Old Testament. This would mean either that the Old Testament is a neutral book, which can fit with equal ease into more than one religious connection, or that it is a comprehensive, germinal book with tendencies that can lead with equal fitness to either the Jewish synagogue or the Christian Church, without giving clear-cut support to either one. Apart from the fact that this solution will satisfy neither Jews nor Christians, it is suspect because it does no justice to the Old Testament itself. This book does not represent a completed revelation. It looks forward to the fulfillment of its promise. It cannot be considered neutral toward what might follow it; its ultimate goal cannot be both the particularist synagogue and the universal Church. To regard the Old Testament as neutral or ambiguous is an expression not of the faith of the Old Testament but of the shallow tolerance of the twentieth century. Those who take the Old Testament seriously will have to ask earnestly what sequel rightly represents its true character.

Honest Jews such as the great scholar Martin Buber say that the Christians have no right to the Old Testament —

it is the rightful possession of the Jews, and Christians show unwarranted presumption when they claim it as their own.

The Christian Church, however, knows that this is not so. Jesus came announcing the fulfillment of Scripture in his own ministry and person. The Apostolic Church preached the gospel as the fulfillment of the Old Testament promise. Paul was convinced that it was non-Christian Jewish readers who had a veil over their heart and mind when they read the Old Testament. When they turned to Christ, however, he saw that the veil was taken away and they could read the Old Testament in its true and God-intended sense (II Cor. 3:12-16). In other words, Jesus and Paul laid clear claim to the Old Testament. If that is not the Church's book, the New Testament is not a trustworthy book. If the two Testaments are not basically a unity, the gospel is not the genuine and God-given message for men. The question whether the Old Testament belongs in the Christian canon is therefore not a minor issue but a crucial decision for the Church.

This decision can be made only in faith and by the theological thinking that grows out of true faith. The Old Testament certainly is an incomplete book. We must not think that the Jews use it as their complete norm, while the Christians have to supplement it by the New Testament. The fact is that from the Old Testament two lines diverge and call for decision. One line, which the Jews defend, points forward to the oral tradition of the Pharisees and its written sequel in the Mishnah and Talmud; it thus leads on to orthodox Judaism and the various forms of Judaism of our day. The other line, which the Christians testify is true, points forward to Jesus Christ, the Christian Church, and the world gospel. Which has found the deep and true message of the Old Testament? Which has grasped the work and revelation of God in its full aim and scope? Which offers the fulfillment and perfection of its essential word to man?

We answer in grateful words that the Church has grasped the truth. We say that the Old Testament, truly understood, points to Christ. We see its intended goal in the Church and its world mission. The Old Testament is a Christian book. It belongs to the Church which confesses Jesus Christ as Lord.

IV

Should Scripture Include the Apocrypha?

THE Apocrypha have long been a subject of debate among Christians. This vigorous difference of opinion still continues, and it seems destined to receive increased attention. A number of recent books have emphasized the importance that the Apocrypha have for Christian study and life. The revision of the Apocrypha prepared by the Standard Bible Committee and now being published by the National Council of the Churches of Christ in the U.S.A. guarantees that the Apocrypha will be the object of increased interest during the next few years. Obviously the Church needs to think clearly and teach plainly concerning the proper place of the Apocrypha in Christian worship and teaching.

THE MEANING OF THE WORD " APOCRYPHA "

The word " Apocrypha " has had a rather complicated history. It is a plural form of Greek origin. At first it referred, as the Greek root would indicate, to hidden or concealed things. It could describe religious writings as hidden or concealed either because they were thought unworthy or, as often happened, because they were too sacred or important to be made known to outsiders or to beginners in

the faith. On this latter view they were to be used only by
the members of the group, or were to be given only to
those advanced in faith, or were to be withheld until a
future time for which they were intended. The word came
to be used to describe writings that were denied a place
in the worship services of the group and so were limited
to private use.

In Protestant study of the Old Testament canon the
word " Apocrypha " may mean those writings which, although not granted canonical standing, hold an honored
place in close relation to fully canonical books. To those
groups who do not concede to such writings a place of distinction as a near-canonical collection, the word is a con-
venient way to refer to this special collection of rejected
writings which others give canonical or near-canonical
rank.

The list of books included in this group has not always
been the same. Luther did not consider the Apocrypha
canonical, but he thought them " good and useful for reading," so in his German translation of the Bible (1534) he
included them as an appendix. His list is not identical with
that found in the English King James Version of 1611: he
did not include I and II Esdras. In the remainder of our
discussion we follow the latter list. We use the word to
mean the books that were included as Apocrypha in the
King James Version.

It is worth-while to emphasize the fact that the Apocrypha were present in the King James Version (and were
also made available in the English Revised Version). The
1957 revision of the Apocrypha may appear to some to be
a wicked departure from the King James Version. The
opposite will be true. The original King James Version
included the Apocrypha. It did not clearly separate them
from the Old Testament by a preface; it did not give a

clear explanation of their subordinate rank. The table of Scripture lessons for public reading included the Apocrypha passages as Old Testament readings. The Revised Standard Version of the Apocrypha will first be published separately. It will always clearly separate the Apocrypha from the Old Testament. This version probably will be available for church use in two forms; one form, then, would contain the Apocrypha, for the use of those churches and individuals who desire such a Bible, while the other would not contain them or refer to them.

THE CONTENTS AND DATES OF THE APOCRYPHA

To most Christians the contents of the Apocrypha are quite unknown. It will be worth-while to name these books and indicate briefly their content. We list them not according to the date or subject matter, but in the order in which they appear in the King James Version.

1. *First Esdras.* This is mainly a free Greek translation of the closing part of II Chronicles, almost all of Ezra, and about one chapter of Nehemiah. It also includes, in chs. 3:1 to 5:6, the famous story of the three guards of Darius who disputed whether wine, the king, or women were the strongest. The dispute ended with victory for the youth who first argued that women were the strongest, and then added: " Great is the truth, and stronger than all things " (ch. 4:35). I Esdras may have been completed in Greek about the second century B.C.

2. *Second Esdras.* In its original draft this was an apocalyptic work by an earnest and honest Jew who could not understand why God had permitted the destruction of Jerusalem in A.D. 70. He wrote the twelve basic chapters in Hebrew (or Aramaic?) about the end of the first century A.D. Christian editors prefixed two chapters to it in the second century, and during the third century added two

chapters at the end. II Esdras survives mainly in a Latin translation of a Greek translation of the original Hebrew.

3. *Tobit*. Although this book purports to tell of events in the Jewish captivity during the seventh century B.C., it is in reality a story composed in the late third or early second century B.C. It is an attractive reflection of earnest Jewish piety and devotion to the Law.

4. *Judith*. Like Tobit, this book is in form a history. It describes how the Palestinian city of Bethulia was delivered from Nebuchadnezzar's army by a beautiful and pious woman named Judith. By stratagem, without violating the law of her people or losing her honor, she was able to slay the general of the king's army and thus cause the foe to flee in panic. In reality, this too is a fictional work. It dates from about the middle of the second century B.C., and reflects Jewish piety of that period.

5. *Additions to Esther*. The Greek version of Esther contained six additions to the original Hebrew work. These additions gave a more religious content to the book, and further glorified Esther and the Jews. They may be dated in the latter half of the second century B.C. In the Greek and Latin versions of Esther they appear as integral parts of the book. In the English Apocrypha the six brief sections are printed separately.

6. *The Wisdom of Solomon*. This book is an outstanding example of Jewish Wisdom literature as affected by Hellenistic thought. It comes to us from about the first half of the first century B.C., and probably was written in Greek. It contains a praise of wisdom, a description of its works, a burning condemnation of idolatry, and a glorification of Israel as the chief home of wisdom.

7. *Ecclesiasticus, or the Wisdom of Jesus the Son of Sirach*. Written in Hebrew about 180 B.C., this, the longest book of the Apocrypha, is a compendium of Wisdom say-

ings on a great variety of subjects. It includes much material on definite religious subjects, along with various thoughtful and sometimes prudential comments on social relations and personal conduct. It was translated into Greek about 132 B.C. by the author's grandson, who describes his task and purpose in a prologue.

8. *Baruch.* Included as ch. 6 of the English translation of this book is the Epistle of Jeremiah, a vigorous attack on Babylonian idolatry. Possibly it was written as early as 300 B.C., but it may be dated at the latest in the second century B.C. The five chapters of the original book of Baruch, purporting to come from the time shortly after the fall of Jerusalem to the king of Babylon in 587 B.C., include a confession of the sin of Israel, a plea for divine mercy, a praise of wisdom, and a promise that Jerusalem will be restored. The parts of the book, it appears, were written at different times, in the first two centuries B.C., but the final form of the book may date from the latter part of the first century A.D.

9. *Additions to Daniel.* The Greek translation of Daniel included additions made in the second half of the second century B.C. to the original work, whose date is about 165 B.C. The additions are: (1) the Song of the Three Holy Youths, when they were put in the fiery furnace; included in this section is the Prayer of Azariah; (2) The History of Susanna, a story in which Susanna is cleared of a malicious charge of adultery, and saved from death, by the acute questioning of Daniel; (3) Bel and the Dragon, two brief stories written to discredit idolatry.

10. *The Prayer of Manasseh.* The setting of this prayer is the time when, according to II Chron. 33:11-13, King Manasseh was taken to Babylon in chains. It was written in the second or first century B.C. It is an expression of repentance and a plea for mercy and forgiveness.

11. *First Maccabees.* For the history of the Jews under the three Maccabean brothers Judas, Jonathan, and Simon (175-135 B.C.), this is the basic historical source. It gives the historical background of The Book of Daniel. While it never uses the word " God," it is not only a hotly patriotic book but also a truly religious writing. Its date of writing is about 100 B.C., or at the latest very early in the first century B.C.

12. *Second Maccabees.* This is not an original work. Apart from two letters from Palestinian Jews to Jews in Egypt, the book contains a summary of a history which had been written by Jason of Cyrene. The aim of the author was to put in briefer summary and in a more pleasing literary form Jason's history of the Jews during the critical years from 176 to 161 B.C. It thus offers a partial parallel to I Maccabees, but its specific references to God's interventions make it appear a much more religious book. It abounds in spectacular miraculous features, and shows great interest in God's protection of the Temple at Jerusalem.

THE ORIGINAL LANGUAGES OF THE APOCRYPHA

Like the Wisdom of Solomon, II Maccabees was written in Greek. Some scholars have thought that the additions to Esther and Daniel, and the Prayer of Manasseh, were likewise written in Greek; others hold that these latter works were written in Hebrew or Aramaic, as were the rest of the Apocrypha. However, apart from the portion of Ecclesiasticus — more than half — that has survived in Hebrew, and some *Qumrân* fragments of Hebrew and Aramaic manuscripts of Tobit, the Hebrew or Aramaic originals have perished. Even the Greek translation of II Esdras has long since been lost.

All these books of the Apocrypha, with the exception

of the Hebrew and Aramaic portions of Ecclesiasticus and Tobit, have survived only because the Christians have kept them. The Jews discarded them, as they did all their ancient Greek translations and writings, and kept no copies of them. Ecclesiasticus remained in use the longest, though it was not really canonical for the Jews, and they finally discarded it altogether. The Apocrypha survived, however, in the Greek, Syriac, and Latin forms used by the Church, and so have come down to us in our English translation. In modern times they have found renewed use among the Jews.

THE INFLUENCE OF THE SEPTUAGINT

How did it happen that Christians could differ so much concerning the proper limits of the Old Testament? How did it come about that some Christians claim that the books that we call the Apocrypha are an integral and fully authoritative part of the Bible, while Protestants deny them this canonical rank? The basic ground for the difference is the fact that the Septuagint did not clearly preserve the limits which the Hebrew canon of the Old Testament established.

We have already traced briefly the history of the formation of the Hebrew canon, and in that connection we noted that the Septuagint was likewise a process of growth. The name Septuagint, which comes from *septuaginta,* the Latin word for " seventy," was first of all a reference to the Greek translation of the Pentateuch made at Alexandria in Egypt about the middle of the third century B.C. The name recalls the legend preserved in the so-called Letter of Aristeas. According to this story, written about 100 B.C., the Jewish high priest at Jerusalem, in response to an appeal from Ptolemy II of Egypt (285–246 B.C.) , sent seventy-two elders to Alexandria to translate the Jewish Law into Greek for

the king's library. Because some ancient forms of the story
gave the total number of the translators as seventy (*septuaginta*), the name Septuagint came into use for the translation. This legend preserves the memory of the time and
place of the translation, but the actual reason for the translation was no doubt the need of the Greek-speaking Jews
of Egypt to have their Law in Greek to use in worship and
teaching.

Later the other books of the Old Testament were translated into Greek, and in time they were included under
the name Septuagint. But these Biblical books of the
Prophets and the Writings evidently were not preserved in
the extent, order, and grouping that were current in
Palestine. These two divisions of the Hebrew canon, the
Prophets and the Writings, were mingled in Greek forms
of the Old Testament, and it is at least possible that in the
first century A.D. a number of other books, not canonical
to Palestinian Jews, were given canonical rank in Egypt.

THE CONTENTS OF THE SEPTUAGINT

Just what this Jewish Old Testament in Greek really
contained we cannot say with certainty. In the first place,
it is not proved that the Jews at Alexandria had a clear
idea of a closed canon of Scripture. That the Law was authoritative is certain, but the mingling of the Prophets and
the Writings, and the use of other writings as likewise
worthy of some special respect, leaves us uncertain whether
these Prophets and Writings were clearly canonical and
definitely marked off from other Jewish writings of value.

Unfortunately, no lists of canonical books have come
down to us from the Jews of Egypt, or from any other
ancient Jews who used the Greek Old Testament. We
know that the early Christians of ancient Egypt were very
broad in their acceptance of Christian writings. Had the

New Testament depended on Egyptian usage alone, it probably would have contained several writings that are not now in our New Testament canon. So it is interesting and suspicious that in the Old Testament also we get evidence from Egypt of a tendency to accept more books than the Hebrew canon of Palestine had. This evidence all comes from the ancient Christians, but if the Jews of Egypt were as broad in sympathy as were the Christians there, and if the broad limits of the Old Testament canon of the later Christians had roots in a broad-mindedness of Egyptian Jews, then we may say that there were two conceptions of the canon in ancient Judaism, one that produced the Palestinian canon which Jews still use, and one that not only included additions to Esther and Daniel but also added other books to those which Palestinian Jews accepted. We are reduced to precarious inference about the attitude of the Jews in Egypt, but it seems that they either had no fully defined and finally fixed canon, or had a wider canon than their Palestinian brothers.

It is my conviction that the Egyptian Jews had no fully defined and definitely closed canon. Philo, at least, held that divine inspiration still continued in the first century Judaism in which he shared at Alexandria. But it is also my conviction, from the available evidence, that the Greek-speaking Jews were hesitant about explicitly widening the limits of the canon.

JOSEPHUS ON THE CANON

In saying this I do not lay chief emphasis on what Josephus says. In a Greek work entitled *Against Apion* (I.8) and dating from the end of the first century A.D., this Jewish historian gives the number of the canonical books. He states that for many generations these had been the definitely separated and authoritative books of the Jews. It is not absolutely certain which books he means. He mentions the five books of the Law, thirteen prophetic books, and four books of hymns and wisdom. This totals twenty-two, the number of letters of the Hebrew alphabet. The usual rabbinic reckoning was twenty-four, but Josephus probably grouped Ruth with Judges and Lamentations with Jeremiah. Thus his canon was close to if not identical with the Hebrew Old Testament of Palestine. He apparently included just the books that we have in our Protestant canon, except that the order of the books was different, and the Greek Old Testament he used probably had the Greek Esther and Daniel with the additions that we find in our Apocrypha.

Josephus, however, was not really a Jew of the Dispersion. He grew up in Palestine; he wrote his first book in Aramaic or Hebrew and then translated it into Greek; and in general he no doubt favored the Biblical views of Palestine rather than those which were current in Egypt.

The Canon of Philo

Philo is vastly more important for our study of the canon among Egyptian Jews. His extensive writings permit us to say something more definite about at least one prominent Jewish view of the Greek Bible. His works all take the form of exposition and discussion of the Pentateuch; he shows that the Law was the basic Scripture to Hellenistic Jews as it was to Palestinian Aramaic-speaking Jews. The vast majority of his quotations and specific mentions of Scripture passages deal with the Pentateuch, but he has occasional uses of other Biblical books.

It surely is highly significant that Philo never quotes any of our Apocrypha as Scripture. He shows knowledge of some of these other books, but such acquaintance does not prove that he thought them canonical. Philo no doubt

thought that the other Biblical books were on a lower level
of authority than the Law; he certainly held that the inspiration of God still continued and had not ceased, as
Josephus and the Palestinian rabbis thought it had, with
the reign of Artaxerxes I; but there is no evidence that he
elevated to the rank of canonical Scripture any book not
in the Hebrew canon.

Until someone brings forth definite evidence that Philo
or some substantial group of ancient Jews specifically assigned full canonical authority to some of these other
books, it would be to the credit of scholarship to stop making the unqualified statement that the Septuagint, which
we know only from later Christian copies, proves that the
Jews had an Alexandrian canon much larger than the
Palestinian canon. No one can prove that they did not have
a larger canon, but no one can prove that they did, and the
available direct evidence, such as the usage of Philo, favors
the conclusion that they did not.

THE CANON OF JESUS AND HIS DISCIPLES

Even if it were established that there were two competing
Jewish canons of Scripture, the question would still remain
as to which of them Jesus and the New Testament writers
used and accepted. There are many scholarly books that
say confidently that from the very beginning the Greek
Old Testament constituted the Bible of the Christians.
This if true would be a highly significant fact. But how
can any person say such a thing? The facts point the other
way. In the first place, no group of Christians accepts as
Scripture all the books that claim a place in the Septuagint. For example, III and IV Maccabees appear in some
manuscripts of the Septuagint, but IV Maccabees is not
canonical to either the Greek or the Roman or the Protestant Church, and only the Greek Church is at all favor-

able to III Maccabees. In the second place, the limits of the first century Greek Old Testament are not clear. No authority gives us a list of the books that were included, and our oldest Greek manuscripts vary in the books they contain. The assumption that the Greek Old Testament was a fixed entity is as difficult to support as is the reference to an Alexandrian canon. In the third place, if the evidence from Jesus and the New Testament writers is to have an important influence on our thought and decision, we can hardly accept this elusive Greek Old Testament as our Old Testament canon.

Jesus and the first Christians lived in Palestine. As a rule Jesus spoke Aramaic, and no doubt most of his first disciples did the same. We know that some Greek was spoken in first century Palestine, and it is reasonable to suppose that Jesus could speak some Greek and that bilingual Christians, who could speak both Aramaic and Greek, were present in the Church from the first. But the setting is Palestine, the prevailing language is Aramaic, and the overwhelming probability is that both Jesus and his first disciples accepted the Palestinian canon of the Hebrew Old Testament. This high probability becomes as certain as we can expect ancient evidence to make it when we find in the New Testament that Jesus, while he quotes many times from the books of the Law, the Prophets, and the Writings, never quotes a passage from the Apocrypha as Scripture. This ignoring of the Apocrypha is what we would expect, and it is what we find. The inference is that the Twelve and the other original disciples followed the usage of Jesus.

THE CANON OF THE NEW TESTAMENT AUTHORS

The situation might be expected to change when we turn from the Aramaic-speaking Jesus to the Greek New Testament. While some scholars have contended that a few of our New Testament books, especially the Gospels, were originally written in Aramaic, the bulk of the New Testament was certainly made up of originally Greek compositions, and it is highly probable that all the twenty-seven New Testament books were composed in Greek. Moreover, the writers of these books knew the Greek Old Testament. Some of their quotations may reflect direct use of the Hebrew text, but the prevailing practice is to cite or reflect the Greek translation.

This Greek Old Testament, we have said, was probably not so clearly a definite canon of Scripture as was the Hebrew Old Testament. It certainly was not identical in content with the Hebrew Bible of Palestinian Jews. Whether it contained added books or not — and quite possibly it did — it at least contained the additions to Esther and Daniel. Such additions mark the beginnings of a process which was finally to lead the Roman Church to full acceptance of several added writings. But this initial stage has nothing decisive in it. To add portions to an existing work is somewhat of a departure from the canon, but until we hear indignation from orthodox Christians because the doxology of the Lord's Prayer, the last thirteen verses of Mark, and the story of the woman taken in adultery have been included in our King James Bibles, we need not regard this step as a fatal breaking of canonical limits.

The main question is not what books the Jewish Greek Old Testament included. It may well have contained not only additions to books but also additional books; we have no specific evidence with which to settle this question. Our real question is, Did the New Testament writers regard the Apocrypha as Scripture? And just as we could find no explicit evidence that Philo or any Jew did so, just as we could find no definite evidence that Jesus or the Twelve did so, so we find no real evidence that the New

Testament writers did. When we examine their use of Scripture, we must agree that certain writers, including Paul and the writer of Hebrews, knew some of this Apocryphal material, just as they may have known writings of Philo. But to know a book does not necessarily mean to regard it as canonical, and we can say plainly that no New Testament writer ever quotes one of the Apocrypha as Scripture. This is remarkable; they have references to Jewish writings outside of the canon, yet they never refer to one of the Apocrypha as a Biblical authority.

If a wider canon than the Hebrew Old Testament was present, we must indeed resort to the lame device of a Roman Catholic scholar who says that this larger canon passed " tacitly " through the fingers of the apostles to the later Church. In other words, the apostles and New Testament writers give no clue whatever that they thought these added books canonical.

THE APOCRYPHA IN THE ANCIENT CHURCH

When we turn to the post-New Testament Church the situation promptly changes. We begin to get definite evidence that points to a rather widespread acceptance of the added books as authoritative. They begin to be cited with introductory formulas which suggest that they are considered to be Scripture by the Greek-speaking Church.

What complicates the question is that this development is not universal and unchallenged. The Syriac version of the Old Testament, obviously under the influence of the Hebrew canon, does not in the early period include the Apocrypha. Church Fathers who know the facts bar the way to complete acceptance of the additional books as Scripture. Melito of Sardis, about A.D. 180, journeyed to Palestine to find out exactly what books the Old Testament contained, and what their right order was. This in itself reflects an uncertainty and division in the Church. After he had learned the facts accurately, as he claims, he lists the books we know from the Hebrew canon, except Esther; but he omits the Apocrypha. Origen in the third century gives a similar report; his own works and the testimony of Eusebius show that he knew the other writings and used them, but his list of sacred Scriptures was that of the Hebrew canon.

These are by no means the only ancient Church Fathers who tried to make clear to the Greek-speaking Church what the original Old Testament contained. As F. C. Porter says, from the second to the sixth century a series of Church writers of the Eastern region stood for the Hebrew canon. Even in Egypt this tendency appears. The famous bishop of Alexandria, Athanasius, who so often is cited for his influence on the fixing of the New Testament canon, states in his famous Easter Letter of A.D. 367 what the Old Testament should contain. He lists only the Hebrew canon, minus Esther. He includes Esther among the secondary writings.

It is important to remember that this is only one side of the picture. The wide and popular practice was to use added books as Scripture. In the West particularly there seems to have been less knowledge and acceptance of the Hebrew canon than in the East. We sense this when we come to Jerome at the end of the fourth century. We must remember that before the pope held a conference which favored the larger canon, Rufinus wrote that the added books were under a cloud and had not been accepted by Fathers of the earlier generations. Later he swung into line and rebuked Jerome for not agreeing with him in favoring the larger canon. But Jerome knew the Eastern Churches; he knew what the Hebrew canon was; and although he accommodated himself as far as necessary to ecclesiastical pressure, he wrote definitely that only the books of the Hebrew canon were canonical; the others were apocryphal.

The echoes of this blunt statement are heard through the centuries of the medieval Church and down into modern times. A series of writers repeat this point of view, and throughout medieval times the tendency to put the added writings on a lower plane than the real canon keeps cropping up. But this was never the official view. Even in Jerome's time Augustine vigorously opposed him, for fear that it would disturb the faith of Christians to have books challenged that they had learned to regard as canonical. The influence of Augustine, and the papal support for the wider canon, largely nullified the influence of Jerome then and in later days.

THE TENDENCY TO COMPROMISE VIEWS

This continual clash of opposing views led very early to a widely acceptable compromise. It was hard to oppose the official support for the wider canon. Even men like Jerome, though they would not reverse their stand so strikingly as Rufinus did, bowed in practice to the official stand. Unable to reject this stand, many did the next best thing. They accepted the disputed writings with certain qualifications.

One position which was proposed and supported was to regard such books as suitable for reading but not for defining doctrine. Another attempt to mark the difference was to call the writings of the Hebrew canon protocanonical and the added works deuterocanonical. At times, however, this distinction was almost erased; it was sometimes reduced solely to a difference of time; the former group had been recognized as canonical before the others, but the difference was given no permanent meaning. Or the former ones had not been challenged, while the latter group had been, but the doubts were supposed to have vanished soon.

In one way or another, usually cautiously and timidly, the tendency persisted to qualify the full canonicity; it lasted all through the Middle Ages to some degree, and in Luther's own day his Roman Catholic opponent Cajetan reflected Jerome's view that the disputed books were not on a par with the books of the Hebrew canon.

This is a curious and tantalizing history. Over fourteen hundred years saw continual pressure to unite the Church behind this larger canon, but the effort never achieved complete success. In fact, given the principle of authority which is inherent in the Roman Catholic Church, and which was a heavy hand on scholarship from the fourth century on, the amount and stubbornness of the resistance, though it was only the action of a minority, are amazing.

Four Main Positions

Out of this confusion and dispute, the modern branches of the Church have come to four main positions, none of which can claim to accept the " original " Septuagint.

1. The Roman Catholic Church, reacting against the Reformation acceptance of the shorter Hebrew canon, made a binding decision at the Fourth Session of the Council of Trent, on April 8, 1546. It rejected with an anathema the Protestant trend. It refused to compromise by giving the Apocrypha only limited authority. It ruled that all the writings we now find in the King James Apocrypha are fully canonical and authoritative, except the Prayer of Manasseh and I and II Esdras. Later editions of the Vulgate print these three works as an appendix to the Bible. Roman Catholic scholars necessarily accept this decision, though their references to the protocanonical and deutero-canonical books keep alive the memory of the different

history of the two groups and show a knowledge of the long division of opinion concerning the Apocrypha.

2. The Greek Church throughout its history has debated the issue without reaching a final and universally accepted conclusion. In practice it has moved toward almost complete acceptance of the Apocrypha; no use is made of II Esdras. However, the lack of a rigid ecclesiastical control of doctrine, and the great influence of tradition and liturgy, have let this Church live without reaching a binding doctrinal decision.

3. A third position is represented by the Church of England. It does not accept the Apocrypha as fully canonical, but it gives them a position much higher than it gives to good writings of outstanding Church leaders. These " other books " — that is, the Apocrypha — " the Church doth read for example of life and instruction of manners." This means that these books are proper to read in the regular cycle of readings in the public worship of the Church. As far as public worship is concerned, the Apocrypha seem to stand on a par with the Old and New Testaments.

4. The fourth position is held by the Reformed Churches. It is well stated in the Westminster Confession, which declares that the Apocrypha are " of no authority in the Church of God, nor to be otherwise approved or made use of than other human writings." This does not mean, as one scholar interprets it, that the Westminster Confession denies " any religious value " to these writings. But it clearly rejects the idea that the Apocrypha are canonical or that they hold a unique near-canonical position which sets them above other good religious writings.

THE CASE FOR THE REFORMED CHURCH VIEW

It is my firm conviction that the position of the Reformed Churches is the only consistent and defensible position. I therefore wish to state the case for this position in a series of propositions.

1. *Other Views Helped by Ignorance of Hebrew.* The vogue of the Apocrypha, and their acceptance in the Latin Churches in particular, have resulted largely from ignorance of Hebrew, which (except for a few chapters in Aramaic) was the original language of the Old Testament. Christians who had to use the Bible in Greek or in Latin were not in a position to estimate rightly the significance of the Hebrew canon. They were bound to be influenced by the form of the Bible that they knew, and to be uneasy about the claims of a different text and canon.

This is clear from statements of Augustine, whose influence was as great as any one scholar in confirming the Latin churches in acceptance of the larger canon. When Jerome, speaking with a knowledge of Hebrew and the Hebrew canon, spoke in favor of the Hebrew canon, this greatly disturbed Augustine. He did not deny the relevance of the Hebrew canon. What worried him was that Christians who had known only the so-called Greek canon or its daughter, the Latin canon, would have their faith shaken if they had to adjust to the original Hebrew canon. The previous period of ignorance made it seem inadvisable to try to go back to the original canon, and it prevented full appreciation of the evidence for that canon.

Whenever the Church loses competence in the original languages, trouble results. One strong reason for the acceptance of the larger canon of the Old Testament was the ancient Church's ignorance of the Hebrew language and canon.

2. *A Septuagint Canon Not Attested.* The Septuagint cannot be accepted as the standard for the Old Testament canon, since there never was, as far as our evidence proves, a definite Septuagint canon. No evidence exists that the

Jews who used the Old Testament in Greek had a definite closed Greek canon which was larger than the Hebrew canon. There is no fixed and definite list of books on which early Greek manuscripts of the Septuagint agree. The idea that a definite Septuagint canon existed before the time of Christ is thus unsupported by tangible evidence. The idea that the earliest Greek-speaking Church inherited a fixed Septuagint canon is a theory without foundation.

We must also remember that no Christian denomination has officially accepted all the books which could claim a place in a hypothetical Septuagint canon. Those who give canonical or semicanonical status to books commonly found in the Septuagint always reject one or more books that Greek manuscripts of the Septuagint include, and the King James Version included II Esdras, which was completed long after the New Testament was written and is found in no Septuagint manuscript. This is not a very clear foundation for a canon or even for giving a favored rank to the added books. To give the Apocrypha an intermediate rating as near-canonical does not agree either with the Hebrew canon or with the hypothetical Greek canon.

3. *The Evidence of Jesus and the Apostolic Age.* For the Christian Church it is of great importance that Jesus, his first disciples, and the New Testament writers give no evidence that they thought the Apocrypha canonical. Our faith centers in Christ and the apostolic witness. Our attitude toward the Old Testament must ultimately be our own considered decision, but certainly the attitude of Jesus and the apostles and the New Testament writers must have immense influence on us, and we part company with them on a significant point if we accept the Apocrypha. The loose talk about the Greek Bible being the Bible of the Church from the beginning is no credit to scholarship. It conceals the very point that is most important,

namely, that as far as our evidence goes Jesus, the apostolic group, and the New Testament writers did not consider the Apocrypha canonical.

4. *The Evidence of the Sermons of Acts.* The sermon summaries of the book of The Acts, and the other New Testament references to Old Testament history and revelation, give no basis for accepting the Apocrypha as Scripture. This is an argument that I have not heard developed, but it deserves close attention.

Those who would give the Apocrypha a Scriptural status, or at least a unique relation to the Old and New Testaments, often say that the Apocrypha must be included to give a continuous picture of God's work and revelation. Only by including these added writings, we are told, do we get the necessary background for the New Testament. Otherwise a gap of many generations yawns between the two Testaments.

This argument deserves particular attention from those of us who interpret the Bible as the history of God's dealings with men. It is natural to infer from this historical interest that the history should be continuous and that therefore the Apocrypha should be included in the canon.

It must be noted, however, that even in the Old Testament period the divine revelation and working are not traced through each year and every person of Israel. That working is found not in an evolutionary process, but in a series of selected individuals and events. All thought of a purely evolutionary process, which would call for an unbroken historical record, is absent from both Testaments. (It may be noted in passing that even if we were to accept the Apocrypha, we still would be far from having a continuous account of the development of faith and ideas in Judaism. Apart from I Esdras and I Maccabees, the so-called historical books of the Apocrypha are largely legendary. Josephus could give us a far better continuous history than the Apocrypha offer.)

The decisive answer to the question whether the Apocrypha give an indispensable witness to the divine revelation in history is given by the New Testament. As we read the sermon summaries in Acts, as we note what events and figures are mentioned there as the Biblical background of the gospel story, we find no use of the men and events of the Apocrypha. What do we find? The span of history covered by the historical surveys in the sermon summaries of Acts runs from Abraham or Moses to David or Solomon. There are minor references in other connections to the checkered history of Israel under the monarchy, in the Exile, and at the return. But essentially the sermon summaries jump from David to the Christ who fulfills the expectation of the Messiah who is the son of David. They show no concern whatever for the period for which the Apocrypha offer some supplementary material.

In the sermon summaries of Acts, the canonical history and books are those which we find in the Hebrew canon. This is a special and striking illustration of the more general point that the New Testament gives no support to the claim that the Apocrypha are canonical.

5. *Persistent Uncertainty About the Apocrypha*. The Church has never had a consistent and convincing tradition in favor of giving Scriptural standing to the Apocrypha. During the early centuries the challenges to the larger canon came precisely from those who knew the Hebrew canon and so sensed the real problem. Throughout the ancient and medieval Church the official and popular acceptance of the Apocrypha was accompanied by scholarly protests against the wider canon or uneasiness at its acceptance. Shortly before the Council of Trent in 1546 decreed that no Roman Catholic could agree with Jerome's insist-

ence on the sole canonicity of the Hebrew Old Testament canon, the Roman Catholic Cajetan frankly criticized the Apocrypha and conceded that they were not really canonical. The Eastern Churches have wavered between full acceptance, partial acceptance, and flat rejection of the disputed books; the 1839 confession of the Russian Church went back to the Hebrew canon, which has been favored through the centuries by a series of individual Greek Orthodox leaders.

We should also note how extreme it would be to include all the Apocrypha in the Old Testament canon. The basic portion of II Esdras was written after most of the New Testament works had already been composed; four of its chapters date later than the latest New Testament writing. To regard it and I Esdras and the Prayer of Manasseh as canonical would be to do what even the Roman Catholic Church has not done. The Vulgate finally put these three writings in an Apocryphal position, placing them after the New Testament as an appendix to Scripture.

One we face frankly the continuous confusion that has attended the use and claims of the Apocrypha, it should be clear that they have no right to be called basic documents of the Church. It never has been possible and it never will be possible to silence valid and strong objections to these writings, except in a Church which can exercise rigid disciplinary power. This inability to get a free, grateful, general, and continuing confession of the authority and basic role of these books discredits the attempt to give them authoritative, normative rank.

6. *Only Strong Authority Can Suppress Objections.* Since spontaneous agreement has never proved possible, it appears that the Apocrypha can be accepted as Scripture only by use of the Roman Catholic principle that the Church is in fact the authority over Scripture. Agreement

has proved possible only on the basis that the Church has the right to determine for all generations what the Old Testament should be. On this view, the contrary usage of the Jews and even the usage of Jesus and the apostles are not decisive, nor can each Christian generation face the issue for itself. The Church has spoken with authority; the New Testament position is not basic on this issue; the Christian must accept the Church's decision as to what books the Old Testament contains.

This raises the question whether the Church is superior to Scripture or the Scripture is the judge of the Church. We must give special attention to this when we discuss the relation between Scripture and tradition. Here we only note that the Roman Catholics have an authoritarian basis on which to defend the Scriptural role of the Apocrypha. Protestants cannot use such a method.

7. *Compromise Inconsistent.* The compromise of reading the Apocrypha in the public worship of the Church, while barring their use for doctrinal decisions, is ultimately inconsistent and unsatisfactory. We can see how it arose. It seemed to protect the true canon, while at the same time it gave a kind of consolation prize to those who wanted the Apocrypha to be canonical. It no doubt made for immediate peace in the Churches that made this compromise, whereas outright rejection of the Apocrypha would have stirred up resentment and division.

In the earlier centuries this compromise took two forms. One solution was to permit certain books to be read only in private. A curious custom was the practice of having catechumens read them. One would have expected the Church to require catechumens to concentrate upon such basic documents as the Gospels and the Letters of Paul. In the Old Testament one would have expected catechumens to be told to read such books as Deuteronomy or The

Psalms or Isaiah. Perhaps they were also told this. But what we hear is that they were told to read certain books that were not in either Testament. This is hard to understand; it does not seem the perfect way to prepare people for church membership.

The other procedure was to read the disputed books in public but say that they must not be used to establish any doctrine. This assumed that for the most part these Apocryphal books would agree with the unquestioned Biblical books. But it also implied that in other points they did not agree, and that in those points they were not to be given authority.

Such a ruling was right in denying full canonical status to the Apocrypha. But it gave back with one hand what it had taken away with the other. What is used in the regular public worship of the Church is in effect normative. It comes to the worshiper with the atmosphere of authority. Therefore this is a strange solution. Free and regular use of the Apocrypha in public worship is a curious way to express their inferior rank. And it is even more curious to think that doctrine is so divorced from the worship and common life of the Church that what goes on in the public worship of the Church has no relevance or control in the theology of the Church. The writings that the Church reads regularly in public worship are in effect its authoritative writings.

To be consistent, the Church must decide whether it considers the Apocrypha authoritative. If they are, they should be used in both public worship and theological formulation. If they are not, they should have no place either in the regular Scripture reading of public worship or in stating the Church's basic theology. Theology is condemned to futility when it is divorced from the public reading of Scripture and the public worship of the Church.

8. *The Apocrypha Add Nothing Essential.* The Apocrypha add no essential to the Biblical witness. They add no essential to the Christian gospel that we have redemption and life through Christ. They are of great value for the study of what Judaism was like during the period from 200 B.C. to A.D. 100. They give helpful background for the study of the work of Jesus Christ and the apostles (as do also the writings of Philo and Josephus and other authors of that time). For scholars they are of great importance, and they can never be ignored in following the total history of the Jews of that period.

But the Bible never professes to be a total history of the period it covers. It does not claim to give complete and continuous coverage of the Biblical period. It is a record of the essential features of God's work with Israel and through Christ and by the apostles. This record serves the Christian Church as the instrument of revelation of the work and will and nature of God. It possesses the power to serve continually as the vehicle by which God speaks to his Church and people. It testifies to God as Creator, Lord, Judge, and Redeemer, and to Christ as the central and sole effective Mediator and Saviour. It lays a claim on men; it exists as a continual challenge to them to believe and obey.

In this revealing, witnessing, rebuking, challenging, comforting, redeeming ministry, made effective in the Church through the working of the Holy Spirit, the Apocrypha have no indispensable role. They add nothing essential. They tend rather to increase the danger of misunderstanding the central meaning of the Bible, for they add to the Old Testament a bulk almost equal to that of the entire New Testament, and so increase the danger that the Old Testament may seem more important than the direct New Testament gospel of the grace of God in Christ. They fail to provide a climax and capstone to the Old Testament in the very thing that is its final significance for the Christian Church, namely, its witness to Christ and its promise of the gospel.

Those who favor giving the Apocrypha a place in the Bible usually argue that we thus obtain a continuous history of events and ideas. But these books, as we have seen, do not really provide such a continuity. The argument may also dwell on the nobility of the content of many of their pages. But in general literary level and in spiritual depth the Apocrypha do not equal the Hebrew Old Testament; and we must also remember that the Bible is not an anthology of great ideas. The Old Testament is a witness to God's work with Israel as a preparation for Christ, and we may well agree with the New Testament that that witness is given in the books of the Hebrew canon. As a continuing witness to Christ and as the needed expression of the promise of Christ, the Hebrew Old Testament contains all the essentials. To include the Apocrypha in canonical Scripture would only increase the difficulty of teaching the Christian view of the Old Testament. It would increase the difficulty of keeping the New Testament dominant in the Church's faith and thought.

THE ISSUE AND THE ANSWER

This is the issue that the Church must decide. As we have already stated, we do not accept the Old Testament canon simply because the Jews did, or even by slavish necessity because Jesus and the apostles and New Testament writers did. We accept the Old Testament as Scripture by a personal and group confession that these writings, when brought home by the Holy Spirit, speak God's indispensable word to us with effective power.

Do the Apocrypha speak the gospel to us with such effective power? Do they speak with divine revelation to us in so central and Christ-centered a way that we must have them in our Scripture? We cannot say that they do. Indeed, we must say that they do not have such power and authority. They are not Scripture, and they have no inherent right to a compromise position which practically treats them as Scripture while maintaining the fiction that they are without influence on doctrinal thinking.

What governs the worship and life of the Church is doctrinally authoritative. The Apocrypha do not deserve that authority, nor do they deserve a twilight position which implicitly grants them that authority. They have their uses; they are not to be despised, but gratefully used for historical study and background understanding. But I must share in the confession that the authoritative Scripture of the Church consists of the Hebrew Old Testament and the Greek New Testament.

V

Is the Apostolic Witness Basic?

To the typical modern Christian the existence of the New Testament suggests no problem. It seems natural to him for this collection of writings to exist and to occupy a central position. It rarely occurs to him that the New Testament as we know it did not take its full form until the fourth century. His outlook differs greatly from that of the Christian of the Apostolic Age, to whom the idea of a written New Testament never occurred. Jesus never wrote anything; he never told his disciples to write down their message; and he never mentioned the possibility of a New Testament canon.

No Immediate Need for a New Testament Canon

This first century indifference to the need or possibility of a New Testament canon is not really surprising. A variety of factors barred the way to the immediate development of such a canon. We cannot blame the first Christians for not planning immediately a definite canon of Christian writings.

1. The basic fact was that the first Christians had a canon. The Old Testament was their Scripture. They had no agonizing sense of a great lack of written documents. The Old Testament was their witness to the revelation of

God. They found in it the story of God's earlier work and the promise of the coming of Christ. They found promises of the realization of God's purpose in the Church. Instead of lamenting the lack of a Scripture, they gratefully used the Scripture they had.

2. It was not only the possession of a written Scripture, however, that at first barred the way to the New Testament canon. The first disciples had a personal center of attention and loyalty in Jesus Christ. They were still too close to the days of his ministry, too much under the influence of his vital presence, to feel the need for documents about him and his work. Moreover, their sense that he was their living Lord was too vivid for them to feel bereft and forsaken. With the Old Testament as Scripture, with Jesus Christ as their leader of yesterday and their Lord of today, these first Christians lived with a sense not of poverty but of privilege.

3. This sense of privilege was kept alive by the presence of eyewitnesses in the Church. Believers were stirred by glowing reports of Christ's matchless teaching, his gracious human-kindness, his powerful healing, his faithfulness unto death, and his triumphant resurrection. It never occurred to them that they could not have a Christian Church unless all this were set down in writing. Oral tradition played a greater role then than it does in our printing-press age. As long as the apostles were living in the midst of the Church, and as long as the witness of the Apostolic Age was a vivid memory, the Christians did not feel cut off from vital connection with the basic message.

4. Implicit in what we have said, and important for a theological understanding of the development of the canon, is the fact that without the apostolic witness the gospel was not yet complete. The report of what Jesus said and did during his ministry was not enough. The apostolic

witness added two things. First of all, it added the story of the crucifixion, the announcement of the resurrection, and the declaration of the exaltation and Lordship of Jesus. Only with these climactic events was the gospel story fully told.

But the apostolic witness is even more significant. It not only attests these events; it also *interprets* them as God's redeeming work which calls for faith. Thus the New Testament revelation was not merely in the acts of Jesus, but also in the necessary apostolic interpretation of that career. This interpretation was not the work of an instant. All the essentials of the Christian interpretation of God's action in Jesus Christ are found in the New Testament. But those first decades of oral witness and Christian thinking were necessary before the decisive writing could occur and the collection of the books could begin. The spoken and written witness of the Apostolic Age forms part of the central revelation of God through Christ.

5. Still another factor barring the way to the immediate creation of a New Testament canon was the strong eschatological expectation of the Apostolic Church. Those Christians lived with the vivid consciousness that the decisive action of God had occurred in Christ. The final order had begun to take form. With confident hope, Christians looked for the coming of the risen and exalted Lord to judge men and to establish the perfect Kingdom in its full scope and final form. The Church was not planning for centuries. It was giving its urgent witness and making ready to share in the great coming triumph. Some passage of time, some sense that the Church must be ready to continue its witness for such time as God saw fit to delay the final Kingdom, was necessary before the formation of a canon of Christian writings could seem imperative.

6. Finally, the gift of the Spirit did much to prevent a

sense of the need of authoritative Christian documents. This was a part of the eschatological atmosphere which thrilled the Early Church. The Christians knew that the gift of the Holy Spirit had been promised to the people of God in the last days (Joel 2:28-32). The fulfillment of that promise at Pentecost was a sign that the Church was living in the last days. The guidance of the Spirit was so powerfully effective that the lack of a new Christian canon was no immediate problem. God was writing the gospel on the hearts of the converts to the faith. What Jer. 31:31-34 had promised was taking place; with joy and eagerness the Christians lived in days of fresh enthusiasm; they felt no need to complain because the new message was not yet set down in writing and recognized by canonical standing.

Such were leading reasons why the Apostolic Church did not begin by producing and setting apart the writings of the New Testament. To note this delay may help us to see that the Church is not founded on a book. It is not even founded on the Old Testament Scripture, for it is clear that the gospel message to which the first Christians gave witness was for them the central thing. The Church owes its origin to God, to his unique, central, decisive action in Jesus Christ, and to the Spirit's interpretation of that action in the witness of the Apostolic Age. The indifference of the first Christians to the possibility of a New Testament canon centers our attention on the revealing, redeeming action of God through Jesus Christ and the Holy Spirit.

The Forming of the Canon a Gradual Process

It was inevitable, however, that the situation should soon begin to change. A process began which led to the production, use, evaluation, collection, and canonization of a group of Christian writings.

It is important to remember that it was a process. Its

beginnings are most difficult to trace, and the effective factors we cannot discern and weigh with certainty. Moreover, it is a most remarkable process from a literary point of view. If we could face the question without knowing what had actually happened, none of us would predict that the New Testament would consist of just such writings as it actually contains. Something like the Gospels we might have expected, for the story of the work of God in Christ would have to take the central place in such a canon. But who would have expected four such Gospels, instead of one adequate and satisfactory one? And who would have suspected that of the twenty-seven writings, twenty-one or, as the literary form of Revelation could suggest, twenty-two would take the form of letters? A process begins, and it is not such a process as we would have predicted.

Factors Leading Inevitably to a Canon

What factors, then, led the Church to form the New Testament canon? There were some that in time would have led to a canon even if dangers had not taught the Church the wisdom of defining the canon for the defense of the gospel. We may look first at them.

1. The very existence of books that contained the basic message of the Church would challenge the Church to rethink its position. At best the Old Testament was but a promise and an indirect witness to " the things which have been accomplished among us " (Luke 1:1). Christians began to write gospels and letters and other works to serve the current need of the Church for a direct statement and application of their faith. They had no thought of writing books for a canon. But Christians came to see that writings that spoke directly to the Church concerning Jesus Christ and the gospel message had obvious advantages over the Old Testament witness. In time the superiority of direct

witness to the gospel facts and teachings would impress itself on the Church.

2. Respect for the original apostolic witness was present in the Church from the first, and as time went on the immense importance of this witness would grow in the minds of Christians. The writings that embodied that witness would gather to themselves much of the respect that the first witnesses had received. The attention to the writings would at first center, as was right, on what they contained. But in time the writings themselves would receive a standing that in part paralleled the unique role of the first witnesses and interpreters of the gospel.

3. A third factor, an inherent theological logic, made for a written canon of Christian writings. God had made a new covenant in Christ. Just as the old covenant had its body of authoritative writings, similarly the new and better covenant established by Christ (I Cor. 11:25; II Cor. 3:6; Heb. 7:22; 9:15; cf. Jer. 31:31) should likewise have its attestation in an even more authoritative collection of writings.

This, as I have suggested, is an inference. It may not have been a conscious inference. But it was an inescapable inference, and we cannot avoid the conviction that it was operative in Christian thinking. If God had seen fit to have his former work and revelation set down in authoritative writings, it was to be expected that his central and decisive work and revelation would find written expression and attestation.

4. This inference was not immediately drawn. As long as the end of this age was vividly expected in the rather near future, need of such a canon for the use of future Church life in this world could not be strongly felt. As time passed, however, and the end did not come, the needs of the continuing life of the Church made themselves felt,

and the value of a written basis for worship, teaching, and life was clearly seen.

5. Coupled with this realization, that a continuing Church needed a specific Christian basis in writing, went the conviction that in some ways the Holy Spirit could work better through the written word than through the oral utterance. Christians all confessed that the Old Testament Scripture was inspired by God. It was profitable and serviceable for all phases of Christian life (II Tim. 3:16). Not only had the Holy Spirit demonstrated his ability to use the Old Testament Scripture for the guidance and help of the Church, but the Church had found in actual experience that it was not a simple thing to discern just when and what the Spirit had spoken through oral utterance.

The apostle Paul had defended the vital place of Spirit-prompted speaking in Christian worship and community life, but he had found that excesses and misleading utterances occurred. So at Corinth and at Thessalonica he had found it necessary to direct his churches to test all that claimed to be Spirit-inspired, and to hold fast only that which proved authentic (I Cor., chs. 12 to 14; I Thess. 5:19-21).

Some writers on the canon say that in the Early Church all utterances of the Spirit were considered completely authoritative. But the New Testament and later writings (such as The Teaching of the Twelve Apostles 11:8) refute such a statement. From the Apostolic Age on it was found difficult to be certain just when an utterance was prompted by the Spirit. The need for testing and selection existed from the first, and in time this process led the Church to recognize certain writings as the trustworthy product of the Spirit's guidance. The oral Spirit-inspired utterance never held the field alone; from the first the Old Testament was a companion authority and it also was the work of God's Spirit. Then as oral utterances came under suspicion because of excesses and aberrations, the way was prepared for finding tested written records of the gospel message a more dependable basis than oral utterances.

6. The rise and growth of Gentile Christianity was another factor that led toward a written Scripture. While these Gentile Christians were no doubt accustomed to oral tradition, they were more remote from the scene of the ministry of Christ. As they grew in numbers they found themselves much less in touch with eyewitnesses than the first disciples had been.

The Gentiles may also have been more used to basing life on written records than were the Jewish Christians, although in view of the evidence of the Dead Sea Scrolls and the recent finds in the *Qumrân* caves, we should not overstress the dominance of oral tradition among the Jews. The Essene-type sect at *Qumrân* had hundreds of Biblical and sectarian manuscripts.

But the more the Church spread, and the more it included Gentiles as well as Jews, the more the situation changed; the eyewitness necessarily played a lesser role, contacts with the original leaders of the Church became fewer, and the place of written documents became more vital. Even among the converted Jews of the Dispersion, the need for authentic writings would be increasingly felt. The Gentile Christians no doubt felt the need even more strongly.

7. A practical experience must have done much to further the formation of the New Testament canon. Many of our New Testament writings were written for single churches or for small groups of churches. These churches found that to read these letters repeatedly was a real help in meeting the crises and problems of life. In fact, Paul himself was obviously convinced that these letters could

serve a wider circle than the one addressed. Whether he himself sent copies of the main portion of Romans to other churches, or whether that practice began in later years, it seems clear that the letter soon circulated outside of Rome. We also know that Paul wanted Colossians read in nearby Laodicea, and he had directed that a letter was to come from Laodicea to be read at Colossae (Col. 4:16).

The demonstrated fact that such writings could speak with power to these wider circles was an influence that would lead to their collection and wider distribution and so in time to their inclusion in the canon.

THE THREAT OF DISTORTION OF THE ORAL GOSPEL

As numerous Christian writings appeared, and Christians could say, as Luke did (Luke 1:1), that "many have undertaken" to produce works helpful for the Church, it became clear that some writings were more important and trustworthy than others. It finally became obvious that reliance on basic written documents was necessary. The Church could thus avoid the confusion and legendary developments which blurred the outlines and denatured the content of the Christian gospel.

This was a sad lesson which only the passing of time could fully teach the Church. But it evidently had its beginnings even in the days of Paul. Whether false letters were actually forged in his name is not certain (II Thess. 2:2; 3:17), but at least preachers who tried to undermine his work were able to enter his churches and sow seeds of discord and twisted thinking among the Christians he loved (II Cor. 3:1).

Thus the problem was not simply that the weakness and vagaries of human memory increasingly created the danger of unintentional and innocent deterioration of the message. Radically false ideas arose and tried to dominate and

distort the gospel. This threat to the continuing progress
and fruitfulness of the gospel was so great and so continuing a problem that we must give it extended attention.
Thus far we have spoken of factors that would have led to
a canon of Christian writings even without the influence
of hostility and heresy. But false ideas hastened and shaped
the process, and so had great significance for the formation
of the canon. We should note four of these dangers which
the Church had to withstand and refute.

Four Dangers the Canon Averted

1. *Jewish Christian Legalism.* The direct danger of Jewish Christian legalism was temporary and was no doubt the
least important threat. The Judaistic tendency from which
Paul protected the Church at large did not die out among
Jewish disciples. It seems that there was later a tendency
to combine the Old Testament with one gospel of Jewish
Christian tone. This in effect did little more than enlarge
slightly the Old Testament. It could not bring to effective
expression the gospel's thrilling newness and its Christo-
centric reshaping of all life. The profound respect of such
Jewish Christian circles for the Old Testament kept this
Jewish Christian message too legalistic in tone, so that it
failed to express properly the gospel note of sheer miraculous grace and universally available salvation.

There was little danger, however, that the Church would
remain permanently on this particularistic and legalistic
Old Testament level. Paul and his like-minded contemporaries had made the universal range of the gospel offer too
clear for that. The real danger was, and still is, the subtle
infiltration of legal and priestly and narrow nationalistic
notes into the Church. Unless a Christ-centered interpretation of the Old Testament cancels these outworn notes,
the Church is kept from clear loyalty to the new and cen-

tral notes of grace and unlimited brotherhood. The formation of the New Testament enabled the Church to keep the role of Christ and the apostolic gospel dominant in its ongoing life.

2. *Speculative Gnostic Dualism.* The second movement hostile to the faithful preservation of the gospel was Gnosticism. This dualistic, syncretistic movement was in the air when the Christian movement arose. Whether it had yet taken any definite form seems doubtful. The first actual Gnostics whom we can name were hostile to the Old Testament. They took over and twisted the Christian message, and it may be that it was the appearance of Christianity that led the potential elements of Gnosticism to crystallize by clustering about the gospel story. This seems to me more likely than does the claim that the gospel owes essential features to prior Gnostic teaching.

It may be, however, that the two movements developed in a parallel way, so that Christian teachers made minor use of current ideas which Gnostics made central, and Gnostics found in the story of Christ the best vehicle to carry their theme of redemption from the evil world of matter.

What is certain is that before the second century was far advanced, Gnostic leaders began to use the Gospels (especially John) and the letters of Paul; they even began to write commentaries on these books to give them a Gnostic explanation. They also produced their own gospels and other writings.

This raised two questions for the Church: Which writings are authoritative for the Church? How can the original gospel message be preserved? The formation of the canon was a clear answer to the first question. It did not so clearly answer the second one, since the Gnostics proved skillful in reading their own views into the Gospel of John and other Christian writings. Yet the canon, when formed, did in part answer this question, for it kept the Old Testament, it made clear that the human life of Jesus of Nazareth is central in the gospel story, and it thus showed that the dualistic view of the Gnostics has no real basis in the Christian message, since the Creator is also the Redeemer and the life of faith is a life in which the whole man, soul and body, unites in obedience to God.

3. *Marcion's " Stranger God."* The third threat to the Church, and probably the greatest challenge, came from Marcion. The Jewish Christians lived in isolation from the rest of the Church after the fall of Jerusalem in A.D. 70. The Gnostics, while brilliant and resourceful, really threatened the Church seriously for only a few decades of the second century. But Marcion, whose break with the Church occurred about A.D. 144, established a Church, formed a Christian canon, and created a widespread rival movement which lasted for centuries. He was an earnest, dedicated man who saw clearly and emphasized to the point of distortion one vital area of the gospel.

For our purpose, his view concerning the canon is of special interest. He held that the God of righteousness, the Creator, the God of Israel, was not the stranger God, the God of grace, the Father of Jesus. Therefore the Old Testament, which witnesses to the God of righteousness, cannot be Christian Scripture. So Marcion rejected it as Scripture and substituted for it a new canon. For this purpose he used the Gospel of Luke and ten letters of Paul.

In his view, however, earlier Christians had corrupted the message of the gospel, and this Judaizing influence had made its way into Luke and the letters of Paul. So Marcion set to work and cut out numerous passages which accepted the Old Testament as Scripture and thus identified the Old Testament God of righteousness with the New Testa-

ment God of grace. The radically reduced remainder of
Luke and the ten letters of Paul constituted his Scripture.

The immediate effect of this may have been to discredit
Paul. Perhaps the second century tendency to minimize
Paul had already begun in the Church. At least it was no
recommendation for Paul that a heretic had used his letters for so twisted an interpretation of the gospel.

But Paul still meant too much to the Church, and his
letters were too well known, for him to be discarded. The
strategy of the Church was wise. It kept the complete Gospel of Luke, but it kept the other three Gospels which had
attained recognition. It kept the ten letters of Paul, and
in their full form, but it added or restored the Pastoral
Epistles. It included the letters of other apostolic leaders
with the letters of Paul. It linked all the Letters to the
Gospels by using The Acts as the background of the Letters, on the view that The Acts gave the acts of all the
apostles. In other words, the Church answered the challenge of Marcion by retaining the Old Testament as Christian Scripture, by restoring the true text of Luke and the
ten letters of Paul, and by adding other works to those
which Marcion used. The Church thus gave a wider and
richer witness to the apostolic message.

It must be recognized that of all the events that hastened
the formation of the New Testament canon, none was so
influential as the action of Marcion. We need not go so far
as to say that Marcion created the idea of a New Testament
canon, but his influence was certainly great.

4. *The Montanist Obscuring of Christ.* The fourth
threat to the faithful preservation of the gospel was Montanism. Just after the middle of the second century, Mon-
tanus and certain prophetesses made spectacular utterances
in Asia Minor and claimed to inaugurate a new era in God's
dealings with men. The Old Testament period was past;

the Christian period that centered in Jesus had ended; the new era of the Spirit had come. Montanism claimed the right to put Christ and the apostolic message on a secondary level. The fresh utterances of the Spirit could override important aspects of the Christian gospel; Christ was no longer central. Here again the Church found, as Paul had found at Corinth, that untested utterances of allegedly Spirit-inspired persons were no trustworthy basis for Christian faith.

Montanism really denied the essential gospel witness that God's central, decisive, and normative revelation and redemptive work had occurred in Jesus Christ. How was the Church to protect that gospel witness without which it could not be the Church? It had to make all later Christian worship, teaching, and life center in Christ and the apostolic witness. Free utterances of the Spirit would not guarantee that result; Montanism was making this clear. The one effective method was to make the original apostolic message permanently basic. The best way to do that was to single out those writings which faithfully preserved that message, and set them apart as authoritative. This would nail down the fact that all later faith, thought, and action must be judged in the light of that central message.

Thus the second century Church had to face the threat of Jewish Christianity, Gnosticism, Marcionism, and Montanism. It is not surprising that the closing years of that century saw the clear emergence of the canon. At the end of the century, the canon was there as a recognized fact, and most of the books to be included in it were clearly designated. Just what happened in the earlier part of the century is not so easy to say. We can only indicate some leading lines that led to the canon.

STEPS ON THE WAY TO THE CANON

1. The natural and clearly observable practice was to group writings of similar character. The four Gospels were brought together into one group. Just when this was accomplished, or where, we cannot say with any confidence. It may have been done as early as A.D. 125; it could hardly have occurred later than A.D. 150. Shortly after this date, Tatian combined the current Gospel accounts to form one complete narrative. He called it the " Diatessaron," which is a Greek phrase meaning literally " through four." He may have made this diatessaron first in Greek, and then translated the result into Syriac. At least, the early third century Greek fragment of the diatessaron found at Dura-Europos on the Euphrates River suggests a Greek original. But the point to stress is that he used our four Gospels and no others. For the well-informed Christian writer Irenaeus (about A.D. 185) the number four is axiomatic; to have Four Gospels is as inevitable as it is to have the four points of the compass and the four winds.

Some have argued that for Justin Martyr the Gospel of John had no such established place as did the Synoptic Gospels. This would imply that in the middle of the second century, when Justin wrote, the Synoptic Gospels formed a definite group before the Gospel of John was added to make the collection of four. But there is no clear evidence for this view. It is more likely that when, after gradually winning prestige, the outstanding Gospels were collected, the Church included the full group of four.

It is important to note, however, that such a collection did not mean immediate and full canonization. It was an important prelude — we might say it was the threshold — of final canonization. These Gospels inherited the atmosphere of authority which the Church had always felt in the words and work of Christ. But unless we say that the first New Testament canon consisted of four Gospels and nothing more, the forming of this collection does not yet give us the canon.

2. Another collection was of great importance. The letters of Paul were gathered together at a fairly early date. That date cannot be later than about A.D. 145, when Marcion formed his canon consisting of his revised edition of Luke and ten letters of Paul. The question is whether Marcion first brought these ten letters together or whether the Church had done so before him. The latter view seems certain. The letters of Paul are known and used by Christian writers at the very end of the first century and at the beginning of the second. So they must have been collected by A.D. 95.

Edgar J. Goodspeed, whose New Testament scholarship has added prestige to the University of Chicago, has proposed a striking theory as to how Paul's letters were collected: The publication of The Acts led an admirer of Paul, who knew Colossians almost by heart, to collect all available letters of Paul. Up to that time they had lain, unused and uncirculated, in the places to which each had been sent. This admirer found letters addressed to seven churches; Philemon on this view was a letter to the church at Laodicea. The collector thus had nine letters in all, since two went to Thessalonica and two to Corinth. He then saturated his mind and heart with the words and message of these nine letters, and about A.D. 90 wrote a general letter as an introduction to the collection. We call this general letter "Ephesians," but as textual scholars know, it had no such address in the original. This introductory epistle was a summary of Paul's message, freed from the local color of the letters to specific churches.

John Knox, now a professor at Union Theological Seminary in New York, added to this hypothesis the conjecture, which Goodspeed has supported, that Onesimus, the slave for whom Paul obtained freedom from Philemon, was the one who collected the nine letters and wrote " Ephesians."

This view of the collection of Paul's letters Goodspeed and his school have brilliantly sketched and resourcefully defended. However, it is a hypothesis that rests on no concrete evidence. There is no evidence that any ancient Christian ever suspected that someone other than Paul wrote " Ephesians." In vocabulary and basic thought this letter is easier to explain as a genuine letter of Paul himself than as the work of another person so saturated with Paul's language and views that he could reproduce Pauline language as though it were his own creation.

Another strong objection to Goodspeed's view is that he has to assume that Paul's letters lay unused for thirty years and did not circulate outside of the cities to which each was sent. This is extremely unlikely. Paul himself directed the initial exchange of his letters in Asia Minor; he tells the Colossians to see that their letter is read in Laodicea, and a letter is to come from Laodicea for them to read (Col. 4:16) . The natural thing is to assume that such exchanges continued and widened in outreach.

Moreover, as H. E. Dana, one of America's Baptist scholars, pointed out, the death of Paul must have furthered the collection of his letters. The churches may well have said that though the voice of Paul had now been silenced, they could still read his letters. That would have led to renewed reading and to a gradual process of collection. It seems reasonable to assume that the process which began in the lifetime of Paul was given further impetus by his death, and that it led in time to a full collection, which was complete, at least as far as ten letters were concerned, by A.D. 95.

The Pastoral Epistles may have been added later, though it is probable that they were known as a part of the Pauline collection before the time of Marcion. He made no use of them; indeed, they did not fit his purpose. But they seem to have been known before Marcion made his canon, and the best way for them to have been known would have been as a part of the collection of Paul's letters.

For the heretic Marcion to use ten of these letters did not recommend them to Christians. However, the Church realized that it could not disown Paul. It countered the Marcionite offensive by keeping all thirteen of the letters accepted as Paul's and making them part of a larger canon.

3. Other definite early collections, apart from the four Gospels and the ten or thirteen letters of Paul, are hard to find. The book of The Acts was no part of a special collection, as far as we can tell, until it furnished the New Testament canon the vital link between the Gospels and the apostolic Epistles. Prior to that it lived a rather solitary life, for its original literary companion, the Gospel of Luke, had been separated from it to form part of the four-Gospel collection, and it might have seemed that The Acts had been permanently discarded. In time, however, The Acts proved the natural link between the life story of Jesus and the period in which the Epistles were written. It thus gave unity to the New Testament. But until that vital role became clear, The Acts was a separate book.

4. The Catholic Epistles were slow to come together in one group. There is no early evidence for such a collection. Even at the end of the second century, only I Peter and I John were able to claim almost universal acceptance. And it was not yet clear that they formed the nucleus of a collection of Catholic Epistles.

5. The history of apocalyptic writings was more involved. Abundant evidence shows that the book of Revela-

tion early won wide recognition. Nor was it the only book of its type to gain high rank. The Shepherd of Hermas and the Apocalypse of Peter also found extensive use and considerable recognition. For this reason some scholars think that these three writings were a definite group which held canonical status for a time. This seems to exaggerate. But it is far from being totally false. In the first generations, apocalyptic writings had a wide vogue. They were accepted as Spirit-inspired light on the future.

By the latter half of the second century, however, these apocalyptic books had lost much of their popularity. The failure of the promise that the end of the world was just at hand may have done much to cause this. The excesses of such groups as the Montanists must have been another factor. The Church condemned as unfounded their exaggerated claims for Spirit guidance. It saw that the vital center of the gospel must be found in Jesus Christ and not in such fragile apocalyptic predictions.

The Shepherd of Hermas, which was said to come from the middle of the second century, was the easiest to discard; the earlier (unfounded) claim that it was by a personal disciple of Paul (Rom. 16:14) could not save it. The Apocalypse of Peter carried an apostolic name, and so apparently had a better basis of appeal, but it never won general support in the Church; this is suggested by the fact that it does not survive except in fragmentary form.

Only the book of Revelation retained a wide, yet partial, hold on the loyalty of the Church, and it had to fight for two more centuries to win a fairly firm place in the canon. Indeed, the fight continued even later, and one still finds suggestions in the modern Church that this book should not be given full canonical standing.

How Early Did the Idea of a
New Testament Appear?

This survey of the tendency to collect writings of the same type, and letters of the same authorship, leads to the question, When did the New Testament become a realized fact? We do not now ask when all our twenty-seven books were finally accepted. We refer to the clear conception of the New Testament canon as a definite group of writings, including both Gospels and apostolic works, set apart as Scripture and possessing an authority at least equal, if not superior, to the Old Testament. When did this conception emerge?

We can make one certain statement. By the time of Irenaeus, about A.D. 185, the New Testament was clearly and definitely present. It then included the four Gospels, the book of The Acts, thirteen letters of Paul, I Peter (almost without question), and I John. Hebrews and Jude had lesser support. Revelation was still quite generally recognized; it soon lost ground, then later regained wide favor.

Only by inference can we go farther back than A.D. 185. It may well be that the conception of the New Testament canon was fairly definite by the middle of the second century. Even before A.D. 145, when Marcion challenged the Church with his specially constructed canon, the movement toward a specific Christian canon of writings was probably beginning to take form. Certainly that development would have come in any case. But Marcion, by forming a canon of Luke and ten letters of Paul, hastened the process of deciding what books should carry authority. He prompted the Church to reaffirm its acceptance of the Old Testament and to add to Luke and the ten letters of Paul three other Gospels, the book of The Acts, three other letters of Paul, letters of other apostles, and (quite widely) the book of Revelation.

The Montanists, with their exaggerated claims for their distorted spiritual utterances, underlined the need to choose writings from the days near the central event of Jesus Christ. We may date between A.D. 160 and 175 the definite crystallization of the canon concept and the first clear designation of most of the books to be included in the New Testament canon.

THE EMERGENCE OF THE FULL CANON

We need not follow in detail the later development, which fixed more clearly the exact list of books. The region of Syria had a curious special history. For many generations Tatian's Diatessaron, rather than the four separate Gospels, was the prevailing form of the gospel story in the Syriac-speaking Church. Hebrews was generally accepted there as Pauline. The Catholic Epistles had little acceptance in Syria until about A.D. 400, and Revelation was in disfavor. But after A.D. 400 the situation gradually changed. I Peter and I John were accepted. Later the four separate Gospels came into general use and the other writings were accepted.

Apart from Syria the development went more rapidly. Hebrews met resistance in the West, which denied that Paul wrote it and occasionally named Barnabas as its author. In time it was accepted as Pauline. Revelation finally rewon its hold in the East and was thus generally accepted. The Church's attitude toward the smaller Catholic Epistles is hard to trace, because of their brevity and relatively rare use, but it became clear that the Church favored them.

By the end of the fourth century there was no longer any wide dispute over the right of any of our twenty-seven books to a place in the New Testament canon. Athanasius, bishop of Alexandria, had already listed precisely these twenty-seven in his Easter Letter of A.D. 367. Various councils and decisions of the West took the same position at the end of the fourth century. Thus the seven books that the Church historian Eusebius, about A.D. 330, tells us had been in dispute (Hebrews, James, II Peter, II and III John, Jude, Revelation) made good their claim to be included in the Scripture. The New Testament canon took the form that it still holds for almost all Christians.

WHY THESE BOOKS WERE INCLUDED

By what tests did the Church reach this decision? Once the process was completed the Church gave much more specific reasons than it could have stated earlier. The reasons it gave were not always consistent, and the later Church may not have grasped fully just what led the earlier generations to make the choices they did.

In the case of the four Gospels, for example, we really know nothing of the thinking that actually led to their collection. We do not know whether the collector or collectors of Paul's letters actually had other letters at hand, and so had to make a selection that condemned some to oblivion and preserved the ones that later were accepted into the canon. Who first saw that The Acts gave the needed link between the Gospels and the Epistles is hidden from us. How Hebrews first got its connection with the name of Paul is a mystery. Nor can we say with certainty whether the omission of I Peter from the Muratorian canon at Rome was intentional, and if so, why that epistle was rejected at Rome about A.D. 200.

If we are honest, we will not claim to understand the early stages of the process except in a general way. We cannot always trust the specific reasons that the ancient Church gave. We know that the objection the West made against

Hebrews quieted down only when the Pauline authorship was accepted. Some strong spirits were ready to accept it as anonymous but canonical. Not so the Church as a whole. It wanted to know who wrote this epistle. When it received the wrong but definite answer, it was satisfied. This does not tell us who wrote it, but it shows that apostolic authorship had come to be essential.

THE BASIC TEST

And this claim of apostolic origin was the essential theory of the Church as far as it formulated one. The New Testament was of apostolic origin. The consent of all the Churches was needed to be sure of this apostolic origin. For one Church or region to regard a book as apostolic was not enough. But universally accepted apostolic origin was the basic test.

This view was both artificial and correct. In its strict form it was artificial; before the Church came to the clear statement of this reason, books not written by any apostle had already gained firm recognition. So the explanation was made elastic enough to fit the situation. Mark was regarded as the Gospel that recorded the preaching of Peter, though this at best greatly oversimplifies the facts. Luke was similarly connected with the preaching of Paul, though Paul certainly had nothing to do with its writing, and its content gives no real picture of his preaching. Hebrews was accepted as coming from Paul, though various scholars had to satisfy their consciences by saying that while Paul wrote it, he wrote in Hebrew and a friend translated it, or he " wrote " it with a friend doing the actual composition. James and Jude were finally proved apostolic by identifying the two thus-named brothers of the Lord with two apostles bearing these names. The Gospel of John and Revelation, radically different in style and thought content, were assigned to the same apostle, and the elder of II and III John was identified with the apostle John. These solutions yielded a New Testament written entirely by apostles or disciples of apostles.

This view, I say, is artificial. It does not always square with the results of historical study. It does not represent the exact reasons why certain books were accepted. Some of them were accepted in spite of the fact that they were not of direct apostolic authorship.

But in a wider sense this view is correct. The Church was dealing with essential facts when it stated this view. It regarded these books as apostolic in two respects. For one thing, it sensed the fact that the event of Christ and the witness of the Apostolic Age were decisive. Writings that were to be authoritative for the Church had to give the witness of that crucial period. They had to come from apostles or from those who could give the witness of the Apostolic Age. This is in fact what the canon gives us. With the possible exception of II Peter, all these books meet that test.

But it was not simply the date that made these writings apostolic. We do wrong to think that the makers of the canon were trained literary critics. They had a historical sense, but their main concern was for content. These books were canonical because they were apostolic in content. Their message was the message, their witness was the witness, of the Apostolic Age.

WRONG AND RIGHT TESTS OF THE APOSTOLIC WITNESS

We may ask how the Christians who formed the canon knew this. What enabled them to be sure that these writings preserved the essentials of the apostolic witness? Did they have a sure standard by which to judge?

1. One answer offered is that they tested these docu-

ments by the Church's rule of faith. If this means that there already existed, before the canon was formed, a definite and fixed creed or confession which gave certainty where the earliest writings were untrustworthy, we must reject the idea. It is true that along with the formation of the canon the creedal confession of the Church was taking form. But it had not attained a form or status that the Church could use to decide which ancient writings to keep and which to discard. The confession was taking form from the Church's use of these very writings.

2. Another answer may be that the writings were judged by a continuous oral tradition which was more trustworthy than the writings at hand. However, we have no knowledge of such a tradition, fixed and above question. Where we find a Christian leader emphasizing a tradition independent of the New Testament writings, he produces precisely the kind of material that we cannot trust.

Papias is the classic example of a lover of oral tradition. But we must remember that he knew and accepted the written Gospels, or at least three of them, and what Eusebius reports as Papias' oral tradition, his picture of the material blessings of the final Kingdom, gives us what no one wants to defend as a true saying of Jesus.

Long before the definite canon appears, the Church was forced to rely on the written records that we know. It had no other independent source of dependable knowledge concerning the Gospel story and the preaching of the Apostolic Age.

3. A third attempt to find a standard by which to test the early writings is through the liturgy of the ancient Church. Liturgy is notably tenacious; once developed, it resists change, and therefore it is a help in discovering traces of earlier times. But the word "liturgy" is used very loosely by students of the New Testament and the

Ancient Church. Fixed liturgies with set verbal form are not to be found in the first Christian generations, and no reconstruction of early liturgies from later documents is reliable. Moreover, the worship and the formal expression of faith in Christian gatherings included, as Justin reminds us, reading of the Gospels of Jesus and writings of the apostles. The later liturgy grew out of earlier worship where the words of now canonical Scripture were formative factors. To use liturgy to test whether the canon makers did well is to reverse the proper course. We have no reliable source of liturgy or theology or community practice that is older than our New Testament writings.

Continuity of Witness Through the Canon

The basic continuity, therefore, between the Apostolic Age and the days when the definite canon was formed is through these very writings. A process went on by which they approved themselves to the Church as the one effective means to continue and protect the witness of the Apostolic Church. This decision was not made by rigid, authoritarian Church government. The process took place before organizational unity reached a stage where it could control the Church at large. Numerous leaders traveled from their own homes to various other parts of the Church. There was free interchange of ideas by visits and by letters. But the canon appeared in its basic form before the Church had a disciplinary system or a central authority which could control the process or dictate the results.

These writings made their own impress upon the worshiping and thinking Church. They came into prominence before the last memories of the oral preaching of the apostles and their disciples could fade away. To the first generations that knew them they attested themselves as in essential harmony with the apostolic witness. As conflicting and hostile voices increased and threatened the unity and purity of the Church, these writings proved increasingly that they were the focal center which could keep the Church centered in Christ, loyal to the apostolic witness, and truly aware of the priceless gift of redemption and power which had come through the working of the Holy Spirit.

This realization was sharpened by reaction to the four threats the Church faced in the second century. In opposition to Judaism and a legalistic and particularistic Jewish Christianity, the New Testament preserved the newness of the gospel, the universal scope of the Church, and the accent on the free grace of God in Christ. In opposition to the speculative, dualistic Gnostic movement, the New Testament kept the Church tied to the actual historical events in which it had its origin; it preserved the unity of God's gracious redemptive work with his work as Creator and Lord; it preserved a wholesome ethic growing out of grace and applying to the conditions of life in this world. In opposition to the challenge of Marcionism, the New Testament preserved the link with the Old Testament, the identity of the God of righteousness with the God of grace, and the full witness of the entire apostolic group to the one gospel. In opposition to the excesses of Montanism, the New Testament insisted that the Church is permanently based on the work of God in Jesus Christ, and that the work of the Holy Spirit will exalt and further rather than obscure or displace that work of Christ.

When we look thoughtfully at the alternatives that confronted the Church, we can see that it was precisely by this emphasis on the apostolic witness that the truth was preserved and the gospel made effective for later generations. By continuously giving the written form of this witness a central and authoritative place, the Church was enabled

The Canon Served As an anchor to keep Church true to apostolic message

to continue to be the Church.

We may be irked by the quite unorganized process by which the Church moved toward the firm conclusion that this canon was a divinely given necessity. Our irritation is probably due more to the fragmentary nature of our evidence for the early period than to the actual variation, real as it was, concerning what books should be included. But the flow of this movement was wholesome. These writings were preserved in living touch with the life of the Church, and they received their unique place only because they proved in continual practice and throughout the entire Church that they could bring home the gospel with ever new appeal and power.

LATER RESTUDY OF THE NEW TESTAMENT CANON

We have spoken almost as though the question were settled for us by the end of the fourth century. That would not be true. We have noted that questions still lingered on in certain places, Syria most of all. We have recalled that the book of Revelation was subject to occasional question even later. We must also note that the Reformation period brought a fresh examination of the question of the canon. This should remind us that in Reformation theology the Ancient Church did not so finally settle this problem that we need not and dare not consider it again.

The discussion in the Reformation period took two lines. Even before the Reformation really began, the revival of classical learning had led to discussion of the canon. Erasmus, who edited the first printed Greek Testament to be published (1516), was fully aware that there had been persistent doubts in ancient times about seven New Testament books: Hebrews, James, II Peter, II and III John, Jude, and Revelation. He freely stated this. But he was a loyal Roman Catholic in spirit, and not at all made for martyrdom, and so when rebuked for his views he made it clear that he would follow the decision of the Church, regardless of anything that ancient tradition might suggest to the contrary. But he made public the facts. Cajetan, the official papal representative who opposed Luther, freely recognized them. The slow and hesitating process of the Ancient Church was never again completely lost from view, although for a period between the Reformation and the rise of modern literary criticism it ceased to play any real role in Christian thinking about the canon.

THE VIEWS OF MARTIN LUTHER

More important than discussion of the views of the Ancient Church was the theological testing of the canon by Luther and others. Luther saw clearly that Christian use of the Bible requires an ability to find the center and interpreting principle of Scripture, and he had his clear conviction as to what that center and principle were. The center was in Christ — in Christ as the gracious, redeeming, justifying Christ; this center gave particular prominence to the letters of Paul, especially Galatians and Romans, and to the Gospel of John; it also valued highly I John and I Peter. Luther's principle was that what promotes Christ, what gives the Bible student a vivid message of the gracious, justifying Christ, is the important thing. He was not much concerned to stress the total range of the full apostolic witness as the Ancient Church had included it in answer to the challenge of Marcion. He wanted the heart of the gospel to stand out, and he wanted the Church to test all parts of Scripture by that standard.

It is striking that Luther undertook no revision of the Old Testament canon from this point of view. In the New Testament, however, it led him to single out and discount four of the doubtful seven writings to which Erasmus had called attention: Hebrews (which refused a second forgiveness to apostates) , James (which seemed to exalt works at the expense of justifying faith) , Jude (which Luther thought was derived from II Peter and gave no clear witness to Christ) , and Revelation (which was not clear and did not properly teach Christ) . These he placed at the end of the New Testament in his German translation. First he listed and numbered the twenty-three books that he fully accepted. Then he left a blank line, to show that the remaining four books were on a lower level. He also emphasized their inferior rank by not giving them numbers. They almost form a group of New Testament Apocrypha.

The echoes of Luther's free criticism were varied and persistent, and they never have completely died away. The latest Luther Bible I have seen still has the doubtful four at the end of the New Testament. But the first twenty-six books are now numbered as though fully accepted. Only the book of Revelation stands under a shadow by not being given a number.

THE VIEWS OF JOHN CALVIN

The Reformed Churches, while they have been explicit in rejecting the Old Testament Apocrypha, have almost invariably accepted without question the entire New Testament canon. Calvin never commented on the Johannine epistles or Revelation, and it is reported that to a friend he once described Revelation as a dark book. But in his *Institutes* he cited the Johannine epistles and Revelation as Scripture, so he obviously had no basic objection to them. To the Reformed Churches the New Testament canon has never been a burning issue; in use, the existing canon has attested itself as satisfactory.

The Responsibility of the Church Today

What is the Church to say today concerning the New Testament canon?

1. It is first of all to receive the canon. It does not create a canon *de novo;* it is the heir of the generations that have preceded, and the first step is to accept its heritage.

2. The second step is to use the canon; the Church makes its test and forms its judgment in the reverent, grateful, prayerful use of the Scripture. The canon was formed for the use of the Church, and in its use by the Church it approves itself or opens itself to change.

3. In the third place, the Church is not prohibited from asking whether this is the right canon. The Church is never prohibited from asking an honest question. In the case of Scripture, which must attest itself in use as the Spirit guides us to hear the word of God in this Book, the decision of former generations cannot close the mind of the Church. The Church must reaffirm or challenge the wisdom of the decision which the Ancient and Reformation Churches have made.

a. The Church may even ask whether it must have a canon. But we stand at such a distance from the basic events, and we need so much a faithful witness which can speak with authority to a listening Church, that it is hard to see how we can ever think of setting aside the canon and trusting ourselves to any substitute. Our faith is centered in Jesus Christ. In him God came to man, and the Spirit today leads man back to that decisive action and revelation as the solid basis of Christian faith, fellowship, and life. We know of no way to keep that central figure and that basic message clearly before us without keeping central the writings that dependably present that apostolic witness.

We need a canon, and can only be grateful that we have one.

b. The Church may ask whether there are other books that should be added to the New Testament canon. It has been asked whether, if some genuine apostolic writing were discovered, it would not deserve admittance into the canon. The possibility of such a discovery is slight. Any newly found and allegedly genuine apostolic work would have to be tested and judged by the canon we have. Moreover, if the Ancient Church did not find a book a basic document, it would be hard for us to find a convincing reason to do so. The canon could only be enlarged by adding writings that the Church has known and used.

So we can only consider whether the Apostolic Fathers and the New Testament Apocrypha merit canonical standing. Read them. Remember that we are looking, not for quotable quotes, but for the authentic, basic apostolic witness to the redemptive work of God in Christ. The longer we read such writings the more we recognize that while they contain some very good things, they also are marked by prolixity, a secondary ring, a later note, and a lower level of spiritual appeal and challenge. No essential Christian witness is to be gained by adding even I Clement, the earliest of them. Much is to be lost by adding the tedium and mediocrity they contribute. They clearly give, not the unchanged apostolic witness, but a later and less powerful word. It would be a tragedy to add any of these writings to the canon; it is no real loss not to include them. (For a statement of the contents and date of the most important of these writings, see the special note at the end of this chapter.)

c. The Church may ask whether there are any books among the present twenty-seven writings of the New Testament that should be removed. Many Christians would like to nominate at least a book or two for such exclusion. But they do not agree which one is to go.

This in itself is a point which deserves much thought. We recall that Luther had a test which singled out certain books as crucial, and to a great extent we agree with him. We must observe, however, that when he ranked the Gospel of John above the Synoptic Gospels he was making the latest Gospel the standard. He put on a lower level the much more wide-ranging and concrete material of the Synoptic Gospels, material needed to give definiteness to the figure of Jesus and to keep him from seeming unreal and remote from actual life conditions. We must remember that, in stressing Galatians and Romans, Luther did not set forth the whole Paul, who teaches much more than justification by faith and speaks often of the new man whom God creates through Christ. We may be glad that Luther saw the power of I Peter and I John. But we may regret that he did not see clearly how needed the message of James is whenever Christians glibly say that they believe but fail to attest their faith by obedient living.

THE NECESSITY OF A VARIED WITNESS

We must respect the theological fact that men are different. The various books of the Bible prove able to speak to the various kinds of men. Though men all have the same basic need, they have their differences and may be reached in different ways. Even the same man has different needs at different times. The variety of Biblical situations, writers, and emphases has the capacity to speak to men with an effectiveness and continual resourcefulness that a narrow stress on a few books cannot parallel. That there are four Gospels and several types of letters and epistles is a theologically sound and significant thing.

The choice of the Church, when in reply to Marcion it

supplemented the letters of Paul with The Acts, the other letters and epistles, and Revelation, was theologically right and inspired. We should be wary of any attempt to cut down the New Testament to suit one type of human concern. The gospel is richer than most of us can grasp. Most of us need it in varied form to wake us up and broaden our horizons. To be sure, one writing may be off the gospel center. James, with its emphasis on faithful living but slight mention of Christ and his work, is one example; another is Revelation, whose burning indictment of evil institutions and vivid assurance of the vindication of God's people includes words that sound vengeful. This may warrant our raising the question of such a book's permanent place in the canon. But if the book makes a positive contribution and other writings correct its one-sided emphasis, the question is not serious.

In any case, it is the living Church — and not the impulsive or impatient individual Christian — that in each generation must make the decision to keep or change the canon. If the Church as a worshiping, Spirit-guided fellowship finds that the New Testament in its present scope gives effective witness to the apostolic message, this reaffirms the canon.

For myself, I see no need to urge a change. The right of free historical study and frank theological discussion continues. In practice we must have a heart of Scripture to direct our Christian thought. Biblical study suggests that (1) in the Gospels — all four Gospels, (2) in the earliest preaching summaries, and (3) in the letters of Paul we will find the essential material for a Christ-centered and Spirit-guided testing of the canon of Scripture. From these we are enabled to grasp the unity of the Bible, to give a place to the other writings, and to keep faith and thought focussed on what is central.

For myself I gratefully accept our New Testament as the necessary and God-given witness to the gospel of God's free grace through Jesus Christ, the living Lord of the Church. I find that my real need is not to revise this list of books, but rather to enter into their historical meaning and to hear God's Spirit attesting the gospel to me and my Church.

NOTE
OTHER CANDIDATES FOR THE NEW TESTAMENT CANON?

The reader of the New Testament may ask what other early Christian writings made any claim to a place in the New Testament. The answer to this question should prove instructive. Almost no first century Christian writings other than the New Testament books have survived. The English reader may consult *The Apocryphal New Testament*, by M. R. James. There he will find an English translation of the surviving portions of many gospels, books of acts, epistles, and apocalypses. None of these is earlier than the second century; none is of apostolic authorship; most of them are later, and some many centuries later, than the second century; and none is of a literary or spiritual quality that would give it distinction or recommend it for canonical status.

Most of these writings survive only in fragments. We find ancient mention and quotation of the Gospel of the Hebrews, the Gospel of the Nazarenes, and the Ebionite Gospel, but we cannot be sure whether the references to them really mean three separate gospels, or whether the same work had more than one name or was issued in more than one form. In any case, none of these gospels made a strong bid for a place in the canon; they were used mainly by Jewish Christians. The Ancient Church produced many other gospels which purported to tell the story of the birth and infancy of Jesus, of his ministry, or of his resurrection and his post-resurrection instructions to his disciples. None of these apocryphal gospels is earlier than the second century. Influential in the later Church was the Protogospel of James, which told of the virginity of Mary and was influential in promoting her veneration.

Apocryphal books of acts were numerous. In one collection Pilate is made into a witness to Jesus. In another, called the Acts of Paul, romantic and ascetic features are prominent; its author was disciplined for forging the work.

Letters to and from Jesus, and other epistles such as the so-called III Corinthians, the Epistle to the Laodiceans, and the Epistle of the Apostles, still survive, but none is earlier than the second century and none has any claim to be included in the canon, although the ones connected with the name of Paul appear in ceratin New Testament manuscripts of later times.

Of apocalyptic books, the Apocalypse of Peter and the Shepherd of Hermas were the earliest and most important. For a time they received considerable use. But the former now survives only in a fragment, which indicates that it was not widely esteemed. The latter, according to the statement of the Muratorian canon (ca. A.D. 200), was written too late to be acceptable as part of the canon.

The mention of the Apocalypse of Peter recalls an interesting fact. These apocryphal writings were usually issued under the name of some New Testament figure, preferably an apostle. As far as we know, the presbyter who composed the Acts of Paul is the only author the Church punished for posing as a first century author or for pretending to write authentic history. But the historical value of these apocryphal works is very slight.

The apostle who inspired the most varied apocryphal literature was Peter. We have the Gospel of Peter, the

Preaching of Peter, the Acts of Peter, a letter of Peter (in the Pseudo-Clementine Homilies), and the Apocalypse of Peter. Several other works were ascribed to Paul or purported to tell of his experiences. Obviously, the Church had enough historical understanding to reject these late and untrustworthy works which carried the name of Peter or Paul or some other apostle. But many of such late works lived on in popular noncanonical use, and influenced the art, architecture, and tradition of the Church.

We should note that a considerable number of the apocryphal gospels, acts, and epistles were Gnostic in slant or were written to promote asceticism or some one-sided interest.

More important for the history of the New Testament canon are the so-called Apostolic Fathers. They are in general earlier than the above mentioned apocryphal works, and some of them have had considerable influence in the Church. We list below the writings usually included in this collection, and indicate briefly the contents and date of each. (A good English translation of them is found in Edgar J. Goodspeed's book, *The Apostolic Fathers.*)

1. First Clement. This is a letter from the church of Rome to the church at Corinth. It rebukes the latter church for deposing certain of its presbyters. Tradition says that Clement of Rome wrote it, and this may well be true. If so, the commonly accepted date of about A.D. 95 may be accepted. The rather lengthy writing is notable as containing the first clear statement of the principle of apostolic succession. It has a developed ecclesiastical and liturgical tendency.

2. Second Clement. In content, this writing is a Christian sermon or exhortation. It is not by Clement, and it is not a letter. The unknown author urges the reader or hearer to think highly of Christ, to repent, and to live a

loyal and obedient Christian life. The date of writing may
be about the middle of the second century.

3. The seven Epistles of Ignatius. As he is taken to Rome
for execution in a time of persecution, Ignatius, bishop of
Antioch in Syria, writes to Polycarp and to six churches,
most of them in Asia Minor. Among his aims are these:
to further the prestige of the bishops; to induce churches
to send representatives to Antioch to encourage the church
there; and to keep Christians from trying to protect him
from the martyrdom that faces him at Rome. The letters
date from the first decade or perhaps more likely from the
second decade of the second century.

4. The Letter of Polycarp. Shortly after Ignatius had
been taken to Rome by way of Asia Minor and Philippi,
the Philippian church wrote to Polycarp, bishop of Smyrna
in Asia Minor, to ask for copies of the letters of Ignatius
which Polycarp had. In reply, Polycarp wrote this letter
and sent it to Philippi with the letters requested. The date
was the early second century, not long after Ignatius had
passed through Asia Minor.

5. The Didache, or Teaching of the Twelve Apostles.
This work contains the famous passage on " the two ways,"
and also gives early reflections of the worship and life of
the Church. Its date is much disputed. While some date
the work in the closing years of the first century, and others
put it several centuries later, it may well come from the
first half of the second century.

6. The Epistle of Barnabas. Shortly before or shortly
after the writing of the Didache, an unknown author used
this letter form (1) to deny that the Jews had rightly understood the Old Testament and (2) to claim that the Old
Testament, properly interpreted, is an allegorical account
of Christ and the Church. The epistle was later ascribed
to Barnabas. Like the Didache, this work contains the

teaching about " the two ways " of light and darkness.

7. The Shepherd of Hermas. Though sometimes dated at the very end of the first century, this apocalyptic work probably comes from the middle of the second century. Its main concern is with the problem of sin committed after baptism. It opposes those who deny the possibility of forgiveness for such sin, but it permits only one additional repentance after the time of baptism. It is a tedious book by a simple but earnest author.

8. The Martyrdom of Polycarp. In this writing, in letter form, the church of Smyrna tells the church of Philomelium the story of the martyrdom of Polycarp, the bishop of Smyrna. This event occurred in A.D. 156. It began a type of literature repeatedly used in the Church to describe in detail the sufferings of Christian martyrs.

9. The Epistle to Diognetus. This rhetorical defense of the Christian faith is not a letter but an address or vigorous apology for the gospel and the Christians. It may date from the third century.

Of these Apostolic Fathers, the two so-called letters of Clement, the Epistle of Barnabas, and the Shepherd of Hermas were the ones that received most attention in the process of forming the canon. But it would be wrong to say that any of them was really canonical for the entire Church, and no modern reader can seriously argue that any of the Apostolic Fathers is a primary witness for the apostolic gospel. On the whole they are a witness to second century Christianity, and for that period they are of great importance.

For the history of the canon, an important fact emerges from the above survey. No noncanonical early Christian writing exists that can seriously claim a place in the New Testament canon.

situation. Rarely if ever is the inherited tradition flatly rejected; rarely if ever does the religious group attempt to start its life on a totally new basis. The usual thing is to adjust the rites and practices of the fellowship to newly sensed needs. Every living tradition has to do this. At every stage it may claim to be what has always been believed and practiced everywhere and by all, but in fact it never fits this description. Change is a continual fact.

This too has its dangers. Whenever change occurs, some essential of the inherited faith may be inadequately preserved. It may even be lost. But the risk has to be run. To live is to adjust.

Jewish Tradition in the First Century

Our present question is this: What is the proper place of tradition in the Christian Church? In particular, since the Scripture holds so prominent a place in the Church, we must try to define the proper relation between these two indispensable aspects of the Church's life. This problem emerged in Israel only after the formation of the Old Testament canon, so we need not deal here with the long centuries of oral tradition in the earlier life of the patriarchs and Israel. We may turn to the New Testament narrative. By the time of Jesus the problem was clearly present, and the New Testament deals with it.

Jesus speaks of " the tradition of the elders " (Mark 7:5). He means essentially the same body of oral tradition that Paul calls " the traditions of my fathers " (Gal. 1:14). It was the Pharisees' tradition, the carefully developed and faithfully preserved interpretation and application of the law.

We may be sure that the other sects of the Jews also had their special traditions; the Sadducees, for example, certainly performed the priestly ministries in accordance not only with the written law but also with their inherited traditional usages. The Jewish people attending a ceremony in the Temple once pelted a high priest with lemons for his carelessness in performing the prescribed rites. Thus even the common people knew and respected the regular priestly practices which were the special responsibility of the Sadducees.

The Essenes also had their group traditions. We hold that the *Qumrân* sect which left behind the Dead Sea Scrolls were Essenes or an Essene-type sect. Part of their traditions is preserved in the Manual of Discipline discovered in one of the caves near *Qumrân*. The provisions for ritual washing and for other group practices at the *Qumrân* site show that this group also had unwritten traditions. And we learn from the first century Jewish authors Philo and Josephus that the Essenes had a number of practices peculiar to their sect.

The Tradition of the Pharisees

The New Testament, however, is concerned with the rabbinic tradition which was the particular concern of the Pharisees. It was the tradition that later took permanent and more developed form in the Mishnah and the Talmud. The attempt of the Pharisees was to preserve in full force the law of Moses. To do this they interpreted the law to their generation and applied it to situations not specifically anticipated in the Pentateuch. It is sometimes said that the Pharisees had a rule for every situation of life. This is not true. They left some things, as they said, to the heart. But they did develop specific applications of the law to cover the full range of life as far as they could foresee it.

To understand the Pharisees we must remember that they gave their oral tradition equal authority with the written law. The full law of God consisted of the Penta-

teuch plus the oral tradition. In effect, since the tradition
interpreted and applied the Scripture, it was in control
and shaped the life of the group. Theoretical recognition
of the equal role of Scripture did not prevent practical
control of the situation by the fixed oral tradition, which
could only be changed by the group of leaders and was
handed down with reverent care.

THE CHRISTIAN REJECTION OF JEWISH ORAL TRADITION

Jesus rejected outright this body of carefully formed
tradition. He refused to include it, as the Pharisees did,
under the description of " the commandment of God "; it
was only " the tradition of men," and so was not of binding
validity or authority (Mark 7:8). In his view it was wicked
to set aside a clear command of the Scripture, such as the
honoring of father and mother, in order to keep a tradition
which permitted a man by a special vow to escape taking
care of his needy parents (Mark 7:9-13).

Paul too rejected the " traditions of the fathers " when
he became a Christian. But he centered criticism upon a
different fault than the duty-evading innovation that Jesus
condemned. Paul condemned the conservative effect of
tradition. It had kept him for a time from seeing the rightful claim of Christ. Jesus likewise saw how tradition held
the Pharisees back from seeing the new truth of the gospel,
but he also noted the developing aspect of tradition, which
enabled unscrupulous, clever people to avoid the unchang-
ing obligation to care for one's parents.

Both Jesus and Paul agreed, however, that the oral tradition of the Pharisees, in which Paul had been so fully
trained, was misleading and harmful to a true religious
relation to God. It was not to be put on a par with Scripture; it was not to be permitted to determine the interpre-

tation and use of Scripture. It was not the authoritative revelation, but was to be subjected to the basic authority of the Scripture itself.

For Christian theology this rejection was inescapable. The control and crown of Scripture was to come, not in rabbinical tradition, but in Jesus Christ. He was the rightful Lord of Scripture. He was the central fulfillment of its promises. He was authorized to give the valid interpretation of its meaning. A right view of Scripture set aside the rabbinical tradition which barred the way to Christ; it removed the veil that clouded the mind of the Pharisaic Jew when he read the Scriptures (II Cor. 3:14-16); it let the Old Testament speak of the Christ.

A Warning to Christians

Before closing our consideration of the Pharisees and their tradition, it is well to clear away a possible misunderstanding. There was nothing unique about the Pharisees. They were not some strange kind of human being which has never existed elsewhere. They were, on the whole, earnest and respected people. They were regarded as good people, and Josephus may be trusted when he says that they were in favor with the people. They no doubt had bad men among their number, and their motives were certainly mixed. Their own tradition, later written down, gives good basis for criticisms aimed at them by Jesus. But the Gospels record no fault of these men that has not appeared repeatedly in Christian ministers and leading Christian laymen. Their mistakes of thought and act were those which are the perennial temptation of earnest religious people. We need to say this for two particular reasons. One is that it may keep us from foolish pride when we think of the Pharisees. The other reason is that it may remind us that by developing a normative tradition the Pharisees did not achieve a proper interpretation and use of Scripture. This fact has a great deal to say to the Church.

THE BEGINNINGS OF CHRISTIAN TRADITION

We turn now from the New Testament criticism of the rabbinical tradition and note the important fact that the Christian movement, which began by criticizing Jewish tradition, at once developed a tradition of its own. As we said at the outset, tradition is an inevitable part of any ongoing religious movement, particularly one that finds its central message in events of history. So we need not be surprised that tradition has played a great role during the entire history of the Christian Church. We must understand the stages of this Christian tradition. We must then define its proper place in the Church today.

1. *The Tradition Jesus Created.* The tradition begins with Jesus himself. He rejected " the tradition of the elders " as " the tradition of men," but he gave his disciples the nucleus of a new tradition. His own words and actions were to constitute henceforth a heritage which his followers must know and appreciate. The fact that he chose twelve to " be with him " before they went out to teach and to heal (Mark 3:14) shows that knowledge of his words, actions, and purpose was to be a part of their later tradition.

He taught his followers a pattern prayer (Matt. 6:9-13; Luke 11:2-4). On the last evening of his life, at the Last Supper, he performed a symbolic action which was to recall and interpret his impending death (Matt. 26:26-29; Mark 14:22-25; Luke 22:17-20; I Cor. 11:23-26). It matters little for our present purpose whether he specifically commanded his disciples to repeat this ceremony. Matthew and Mark and the shorter text of Luke know of no such command, and Paul's reference to it could be the explication rather than the quotation of Jesus' intent. But the main fact is that Jesus did this action so that his disciples would remember it and so would understand his death and explain it aright. It was a consciously willed addition to the tradition.

Although Jesus rejected the rabbinical " tradition of the elders," he preserved and interpreted afresh the Old Testament. He found in it a divine revelation, but in a form that called for sifting. He cleared away outworn and misleading features and deepened and purified the meaning (see Matt. 5:17-48). He spoke " as one who had authority, and not as their scribes " (Matt. 7:29). From the first his interpretation of the Scripture was authoritative for his followers; it became at once a part of the tradition that went forth from him.

Not only his interpretation of Scripture, but also his teaching on other subjects, had authority for his disciples. The basis of the New Testament canon and of the Christ-centered interpretation of the Old Testament emerges in his teaching and life as well as in his death, resurrection, and exalted Lordship. To his followers he was the supreme teacher, the supreme interpreter of Scripture, and the supreme example of life and suffering, as well as the Redeemer and the victor over death. He left a tradition that could never leave the Church permanently satisfied with the Old Testament as its sole Scripture. This tradition subjected the Old Testament to him, to his message and work.

2. *The Oral Apostolic Witness.* The second stage of Christian tradition was the purely oral stage of the apostolic witness. There are scholars who say that even while Jesus was teaching, hearers took down notes or went away to write down at once his key sayings. There is no evidence of this; there is little likelihood that it happened. The first

reports about Jesus were oral reports. The Church began with a basic oral tradition.

The importance of that apostolic tradition needs to be stressed. It was not a mere repeating of what Jesus had said plus a bare report of what he had done. It had a wider scope. It included these reports and it pointed out how central and significant such events were for the hearers. But it did two other crucial things. It interpreted the meaning of these acts and teachings of Jesus. And it told as fact what Jesus could only indicate as promise. For it stressed the cross and resurrection and exaltation and Lordship of Christ. The preaching apostle of the postresurrection period had a vantage point quite different from that of Jesus teaching by the Sea of Galilee. He proclaimed as crucial and redemptive fact what Jesus did in his death and afterward.

We often hear Paul blamed because he did not repeat the message of Jesus just as his Master had taught it. Such critics forget that Jesus had been rejected; he was a matchless teacher, a great healer, and a noble example, but he had been rejected. How, then, could his followers think that clear teaching alone would save the world? It is hard to understand the view that Paul should have repeated Jesus' teaching ministry without addition or interpretation. The fact is that the gospel was not complete, the revelation had not really been made in its deepest range, until the cross, resurrection, and exaltation had occurred, had found interpretation in the apostolic preaching, and had been presented as a message of hope to men.

The apostolic preaching thus forms part of the central event of God's revelation in Jesus Christ. That is why the New Testament had to have not only a Gospel section but also, in the Gospels, and especially in the rest of the books, a definite report of the apostolic witness. The task of the apostles and their Christian contemporaries was not merely to report a message. They had not only to proclaim decisive events, but also to give their interpretation. Their proclamation of the events included the interpretation. The apostolic witness was a part of the central revelation.

This calls attention to the immense importance and the unique role of the apostles. Their task belonged to that first generation, which had seen Christ's earthly work and could witness to its full scope and its deep meaning for faith. No later generation could parallel this work. No successors could duplicate what they did. The apostolic witness was the living and permanently basic gospel. It was not only authoritative for the hearers of the apostles, but would remain authoritative for following generations.

We often hear of successors of the apostles. In their basic apostolic function they had no successors. Others took up their message and carried forward their work. We thank God for that, and we praise every later Church leader who proved faithful. But those later leaders did not repeat or rival the unique work of the apostles, who gave to the Christian witness the classic form which was to be the heritage of the Church for all time to come.

What the leaders of that first generation gave as oral witness was a vital stage of the Christian tradition. They handed on the basic sayings and works of Jesus; they reported the full scope of his career; and they provided the essential interpretation which made the story the gospel for all men.

3. *The Writing of the Apostolic Witness.* The third stage of the Christian tradition was the process of writing the apostolic witness in permanent form. This began while the interpretation of the event of Christ was still under way. The written form was determined not by what promised to give future literary prestige, but by the current

needs of the Church. It grew out of oral preaching and teaching; the letters in particular were a necessary substitute for oral teaching; the writings aimed to meet the needs of the Christians of the apostolic and postapostolic ages.

There was no intent to change the witness. Quite the contrary. The writers wrote their witness to help the Church and meet its needs, but they definitely intended to preserve the essential content of the original oral message. It may be argued that the message underwent changes through the selection and shaping of material, through adapting it to the actual needs of Christians, and through the restatement of it to make it fully intelligible to people of non-Jewish and non-Palestinian backgrounds. Such changes, as far as they occurred, were as common in the changing conditions of the oral witness as in its written form. It is fair to say, however, that the essentials of this message were faithfully preserved in the written form to which we are heirs.

The writing of the witness was not a capricious or needless thing. To be sure, a few Roman Catholic apologetes have defended their oral tradition by saying that Jesus never told the disciples to write anything; he only told them to preach. This statement is true, but when thus used, as the German scholar H. J. Holtzmann said nearly a century ago, it proves much too much. It suggests that the New Testament writers violated specific instructions and did what was definitely wrong. Not even those apologetes really meant to say that. To them as to us the New Testament is Scripture, and they cannot deny the essential place of written records in the life of the Church. But the New Testament authors did not write merely for later centuries.

There is, of course, great truth in the words of Irenaeus: " What they then preached they afterward by the will of God delivered to us in writings as the foundation and future pillar of the Church " (*Adv. Haer.* III.1) . But the initial fact was that writing had become a necessity before the Apostolic Age had ended. It was necessary to meet the needs of those first generations of Christians. With the passing of time, the growth of the Church, the dwindling of the number of eyewitnesses, the need for documents to help the new leaders, and the continual rise of new problems in worship and daily life, the first century Church already needed such written works as the Gospels, The Acts, the Letters, and the books of prophecy and hope. In meeting these immediate needs the writers produced the durable written form of the apostolic witness.

This was a far-reaching step in the history of the Christian tradition. There was still no thought of a New Testament canon, but the writings for it took form in living touch with the life and needs of the Church.

4. *The Growing Importance of the Written Witness.* The fourth stage followed, in which both the written testimony and the oral witness were handed on side by side. We lack sufficient evidence to enable us to trace this double process. It began as soon as writing began, and continued after the New Testament books were all written. In this stage Scripture and tradition were not yet competing as they later did for the controlling role in the Church. The New Testament canon was not yet established. Christ, and the gospel of God's work through him, was the normative center of attention, in the light of which the Old Testament was interpreted. This Christian message made its appeal in both oral and written expression. And we must remember that since numerous Christians could not read, they had to receive the gospel in oral form, either in the ongoing oral apostolic witness or in the public reading of writings that contained that witness.

Before many decades the importance of the written witness became clear. It may be objected that in the middle of the second century Papias still praised the superior worth of the oral tradition, which he traced back to the apostles through trustworthy intermediaries, the elders. But, as we have noted, he does not mean to displace the Gospels, which he values highly. He was rejecting heretical traditions rather than trying to keep the Christian witness in purely oral form. And when we read the surviving fragments of his oral Christian traditions, he provides, whether with or against his consent, a powerful argument for the necessity of written records. What he is able to report through oral channels of tradition is obviously late and legendary material. It makes us well content with the written New Testament.

Even less impressive than Papias is the series of gospels, epistles, books of acts, and apocalypses that come to us from the second century or later. They often are obviously warped by heretical distortions. They offer little or nothing that any sane scholar would rank with the canonical writings. It becomes clear that by the middle of the second century the Church had no trustworthy contact with the original apostolic witness except through the Gospels and the other New Testament books. In this testing period, when there was still no New Testament canon and Christians were using both written works and oral tradition, the need for the canon became more and more apparent. The Old Testament alone could not control the rank growth of oral tradition. The oral tradition offered no reliable supplement or correction to the written witnesses to the gospel. Later writings were obviously greatly inferior to the first century documents. The Church had to turn to these early books to give a solid basis for its continuing life.

   5. *Later Tradition Made Subject to the Apostolic Wit-*

ness. The fifth stage of Christian tradition is the canonical period. It began about A.D. 160 to 175 and continues still in our day. The basic idea and the essential nucleus of the canon were present from the latter part of the second century.

Many writers consider this formation of the canon a confession of the Church's mediocrity and failure. The implication seems to be that a vigorous and effective Church would not have stooped to so mechanical, cramping, and secondary a thing as the canon. It would have retained its freedom; it would have advanced by its immediate grasp of the gospel and by the mature guidance of the Spirit.

This is a misreading of history. It is true that the second and third century Christians were not Peters and Pauls. Christ was unique, a once-for-all event. The apostles were great, not because they were the supermen of all time, but because they had a great position, a great impetus from the risen Christ, and a message that gripped them. The later Church was not in a position to duplicate their stirring apostolic ministry. But Christians were to keep and hand on the gospel; they were to attest it by their words and life. Their question was where they could find that gospel, and how best it could continue to do its full work through the Spirit. They learned by experience that these writings were their only hope. They had no practical alternative but to make them basic and normative.

The late second century Church thus subjected all tradition to the written apostolic witness. This was a practical necessity. It was also a theologically sound step. It expressed the absoluteness of the work of God in Jesus Christ; it affirmed the authenticity of the witness of the Apostolic Church. This written witness not only recorded the decisive events of God's action; it also gave the basic interpretation of those events; it furthermore served continually to reveal God's ways and will to the ongoing Church.

This decision did not enslave the Church. Nor was it a radical innovation. The Church had always had a Scripture, our Old Testament. It also had necessarily given the apostolic witness the central role. The formation of the New Testament gave the Church the full Scripture for use in worship under the guidance of the Holy Spirit. It offered a solid basis for faith and worship, for teaching and life. It provided a resource which enabled the Church to discern the folly of the distortions and corruptions that threatened the Church. It built a defense against the encroaching confusion and the progressive fading of the oral gospel tradition.

The canon thus gave each succeeding generation the closest possible contact with the crucial Apostolic Age. The living Lord, the Holy Spirit, the dependable apostolic witness in the Scripture — these gave the Church no sense of slavery, but a sense of freedom and privilege. The canon did not have to mean — though it always could mean — legalism, formalism, archaism, and irrelevance. It was the ever available point where the living and active Word of God could speak to the worshiping Church in instruction and rebuke, in comfort and encouragement, in contemporary power, and with an adequate word for all areas of life.

FOUR VIEWS OF THE ROLE OF TRADITION

From the very nature of life it must be clear that the formation of the canon could not stop the growth or influence of tradition. This gives rise to the specific problem that sets Protestants and Roman Catholics at variance. Though the full Scripture now existed, tradition was present too, and it continued to develop. What is the true relation of Scripture and tradition? The Church can never escape this question. There are at least four answers to it.

1. *Scripture Must Give Way to Living Tradition.* One idea, rarely expressed in any clear way, interprets the Scripture as a primitive expression which should be outgrown and discarded for more mature forms of life and thought. The Scripture may be accepted as a legitimate first stage of spiritual development. But the Church should gradually become emancipated from such an imperfect expression of the Christian faith.

This view tends to make later tradition sovereign. What is later is more mature. Tradition therefore should displace Scripture, whose canonicity, on this view, is only a temporary accommodation to immaturity. This accents the progressive, independent nature of tradition, but it is fatal to the basic affirmation of the Church that the gospel centers in an ancient historical event and its apostolic interpretation. Christianity in any recognizable form would disappear if this view were to prevail. The problem of Scripture and tradition is not here conceived in truly Christian terms.

2. *Selected Earlier Tradition as Normative as Scripture.* A second answer to this question is to assign authority not only to Scripture but also to selected earlier areas of tradition. The tradition of our own day is thus subject not only to Scripture, but also to those earlier aspects of tradition which have recognized authority for later Christian generations. The Greek Church tends to such a view. It regards certain areas of tradition as equally authoritative with Scripture. The decisions and creeds of several ancient councils and also of selected later synods are considered normative. One sometimes gets the impression that even in a wider sense the Greek Church gives a respect to tradition that comes close to putting it on a par with Scripture.

The effect of this is to minimize the work of both the

apostolic witnesses and the writers of the New Testament. It tends to broaden the period of decisive revelation to cover a major portion of Christian history. This is not a sound view. The redemptive work of God and the needed revelation of God are so adequately presented in the apostolic witness that all later testimony is secondary and derivative and therefore not equal to Scripture.

It may seem incorrect and offensive to say that many Protestants have done exactly what the Greek Church has done. We cannot say that Protestant denominations by official action have clearly done this. But the tendency has been present in Protestant writings and groups. It appears in three forms.

a. Very often the first five or the first three centuries of the Church have been taken as a pure and acceptable period of Christian witness; or at least the actions of the great Church councils have been accepted as authoritative for all later Christians. The classic confessions and creeds, the doctrinal decisions of these centuries, have been regarded as practically canonical. This tendency, when clearly present, assigns to this area of Church tradition an authoritative role in later Church history.

b. A second form of Protestant surrender to authoritative tradition is acceptance of Reformation actions as above challenge. A quotation from Luther or Calvin is considered a final argument. The less genial and captivating nature of Calvin may have spared him from the excessive adulation sometimes shown toward Luther, who has even been hailed as "*divus*" (divine). Such adjectives should not be pressed, but they point up the fact that at times in Lutheran and Reformed and Methodist history the words of the Reformation leaders have been given an authority practically equal to Scripture.

c. Closely related to this high regard for Reformation

leaders is the attitude of unconditional loyalty to one's own creed or confession — the Augustana Confession or the Westminster Confession or some other. Such unqualified loyalty to a creed is no longer common, but it has existed and can still be found. It can lift the creed to a rank equal with Scripture.

Such estimates of tradition reject basic Protestant principles. They deny in effect the validity of the canon. If we accept the centrality and finality of God's action in Christ and find the central revelation in the apostolic witness, we cannot rightly set any other period of God's working or any other witness to God's gospel on the same level with the New Testament. Every later confession and decision of the Church must be tested by the basic gospel and revelation which the Scripture itself contains. Not even the Apostles' Creed or the earliest Church creeds can provide an exception to this statement. These creeds aim to express the apostolic witness in its core and meaning. But none of them — not even the so-called Apostles' Creed, whose earliest form dates from the middle of the second century and whose present form arose much later — is equal with Scripture. We can use such early confessions as an important formulation of the heart and meaning of Scripture. But this means that we must test them by Scripture; we must not give even these high points of Church tradition a rank equal to the canon.

3. *Tradition as Authoritative as Scripture.* In what we have just said we have already taken our position toward the third proposed solution of the problem of Scripture and tradition. We have rejected the idea that Scripture is something to be outgrown. We have set aside the idea that some specific phase of Church tradition can be set beside Scripture as an equal authority for present-day Church life. But the third view of the place of tradition in the life of

the Church is more radical and far-reaching. It is the Roman Catholic contention that authoritative guidance and control for Christian faith and life always has been and always will be twofold: Scripture and ongoing tradition.

The clear official statement of this position was made at the fourth session of the Council of Trent on April 8, 1546. It was undoubtedly an answer to the Reformation, for one of Luther's famous theses was that it is sacrilegious to make the authority of tradition equal to that of the Scripture. However, this very thesis of Luther shows that the Roman Catholic position was no innovation of the Council of Trent. It was a position that had been asserting itself for centuries in the Church. It may well be true, as G. L. Prestige concluded on the basis of a careful study of the ancient Church Fathers, that those Fathers gave the Scriptures the primacy and looked to them to give authoritative guidance to the Church. But the tradition of the Church began early to seek close control over the interpretation of the Bible, and it increasingly won a place of independent authority on a par with Scripture. The Council of Trent only formalized and made permanent a reality which had long been present.

We still have not stated the real meaning of this decision. The main significance of this recognition of tradition is that it sanctioned the tradition of the Roman Church. That Church claimed that through continuous, divinely given, and infallible leadership it had preserved this tradition and held it in trust. The theory is that Jesus Christ gave it to his apostles, and they handed it down through this continuous line of papal leaders. A Roman Catholic scholar may have to say, as one actually did, that in part the tradition passed tacitly through the hands of the apostles; in other words, for many parts of it there is no trace that any apostle or apostolic writer ever heard of it. This makes the situation clear. The Church is here made absolute. It says what the tradition is. Nor is the Church brought under judgment by Scripture. On the contrary, the Church not only controls tradition; it is also the judge of Scripture. It determines what the right interpretation is. No interpretation that goes against what " Mother Church " teaches can be right.

In fact, therefore, we have here three authorities: the Bible, the tradition, and the Church, and the primacy is in the hands of the Church. The Roman Catholic Church controls both the tradition and the interpretation of the Bible. It should also be obvious since the Vatican Council of 1870 that when the pope, as the infallible head of the Church, speaks ex cathedra, he speaks the last word on both tradition and the meaning of the Bible.

This constitutes a far-reaching decision as to the meaning of tradition and its relation to the Bible. In the ancient Church Fathers the tradition was meant to recognize and interpret the Bible, so that the Bible remained the really normative authority. The intent of such tradition was basically conservative; it tried to preserve the message and prestige of Scripture. But the developing aspect of tradition has gained the practical ascendancy in modern Roman Catholic practice.

The Roman Catholic doctrine of tradition has tended more and more to become what H. J. Holtzmann said in 1859 it was becoming. It has become a theory of continuous inspiration, which can develop and impose practices and doctrines that have little or no basis in Scripture. Even in the Council of Trent the discussion at times seemed impatient with the testing of all doctrine and practice by the standard of Scripture. There was a desire for the Church to develop more freely whatever doctrine seemed necessary for the growth and dominance of the Roman Catholic Church.

It was not unexpected, therefore, when the bodily assumption of Mary was promulgated in 1950 as a binding doctrine to which every Roman Catholic must give assent. This doctrine was made obligatory even though it has no Biblical basis. This was the clear proof that for the Roman Catholic Church tradition is not subject to Scripture. It is subject to the Church, that is, to the pope, who is wise enough to consult key members of the hierarchy before he promulgates any such doctrine. The Bible can be ignored or overridden by the tradition, and the tradition is a developing quantity which is under the control of the Church.

For reasons profoundly important, the Protestant Church cannot accept this point of view, which blurs the sense of the absolutely unique first century work of God in Jesus Christ. In theory it does not do so. No doubt one can find general Roman Catholic approval for the statement of Thomas Aquinas that " the sole rule of faith is the canonical Scripture." But Aquinas meant " the Scriptures according to the teaching of the Church, which has sound understanding of them." He did not deny the role of tradition or its control by the Church. So the Roman Catholic Church in practice claims that its authority is above rebuke; in practice it sanctions such non-Biblical innovations as granting to Mary a role parallel to Christ in effecting salvation. The central role of Jesus Christ, the direct and decisive relation of the individual believer to him through faith, do not receive their due. We have to say plainly that the Church does not possess or do anything today that enables it to control salvation or to alter the gospel message. The true Church humbly and repentantly accepts from God, as a result of the work of Christ, the gifts which it has no right to control or obscure.

To give decisive authority to the Church and its tradition calls in question the adequacy and effectiveness of the apostolic witness. By the apostolic witness I mean that which is recorded in the New Testament. There is no other source that is dependable. The traditions of the Church, taken as a whole, can make no historical claim to be apostolic. The subtle effect of the expansion of tradition and of its growth in authority is to lessen the role of the apostolic witness and to cast a shadow on its sufficiency, without giving anything that can substitute for it.

Such magnifying of the authority of Church and tradition constitutes in effect a challenge to the canon. The canon becomes a phase of the Church's total tradition, and loses its dominant role. We have seen that in a true sense the canon is the written deposit of the apostolic tradition. In fact, it is the only trustworthy record of that apostolic tradition. It was made the canon because the Church found that as the apostles passed away and their hearers died, these writings became the only dependable witness to the gospel message. The Church faced a crisis. If it was to preserve the apostolic witness and live by it, it had to give these books a place that would control all its faith and life. No other authoritative basis for future faith and life was available. To forget the lesson of that crisis, to give the later developments of tradition a position theoretically equal and practically superior to Scripture, and to give the Church full control of both the tradition and the interpretation of the Scripture, without recognizing that Scripture rebukes and condemns the Church for its faults, is in effect to deny the canon its right to exist.

This Roman Catholic view of tradition and of the supremacy of the Church loses the freedom, simplicity, directness, and purity of the gospel. In this view the Church really consists of the hierarchy. The common people are dependents. They may read the Bible in an approved version and within the limits of a predetermined interpretation. They must accept the statement of their Church as to what the Bible means and what the tradition says. It should be noted that the Roman Catholic Church has never codified or listed its traditions. They are what the Church at any time says they are, just as Scripture means only what the Church says it means.

This is not the gospel of the free grace of God offered to whoever sincerely believes in Christ and accepts in gratitude the gift of life to repentant souls. The gospel message has its best chance of coming through to men when it is set free from the shackles of tradition and ecclesiastically dictated interpretation, and is given to men to read and study and teach under the guidance of the Holy Spirit. The Bible was not meant to be used as part of a system that keeps the mass of church members in the permanent position of immature wards of the Church. It does its work only when it challenges believers to grow up in responsible faith and loyalty to Christ as he meets us in the apostolic witness.

4. *The Protestant View of Tradition.* It may have seemed that we are trying to eliminate tradition from the life of the Protestant Church. We could not do so if we tried. Every religious group always has had and always will have its tradition. The question for the Christian can only be how much authority he will attach to the tradition he inherits and holds.

We begin with tradition. We receive our first Christian training in homes which share a tradition and in a Church which witnesses to the tradition that it considers most faithful to the gospel. We receive the Bible by the act and witness of our Church. We learn the basic features of

Christian teaching and the common practices of Christian worship as we receive the training the Church gives and as we share in worship according to the pattern the Church hands on to us. As we advance, we find that the Church has had a long history, and that there have been earnest and intelligent Christian believers and leaders in every century. We do not begin by wholesale denial of all that Christians have believed and thought. We begin with tradition, and we never live without it.

The only question to decide is whether this tradition is above challenge and must be accepted without dispute. For two reasons we cannot take such a position. In the first place, Christian faith does not consist in accepting Church-controlled tradition without question, even when it is the central Christian heritage that the Church hands us. In Christian faith we face the Christ who is central in the Christian message. We respond to God in faith when we see that in Christ God is claiming our lives and is offering us the forgiveness, power, and fellowship without which true life is impossible. No Church tradition can substitute for this act of faith and continual dedication; no Church tradition can keep us from this simple act of trust and commitment.

In the second place, we cannot let the later traditions of the Church take an equal rank with Scripture, because we believe that the act of God in Christ is central, that the apostolic witness to the gospel is decisive, and that the Bible is the unique means through which that witness comes to us.

We use our traditions gratefully. We receive the Christian gospel through the witness and traditions of the Church. We are indebted not only to the Christian friends of our own day, but also to the witness and ministry of earlier generations which have had a part in making it possible for us to know and receive the gospel. We limited and fallible Christians use their gifts with gratitude; we learn from good men of every century things that help us to understand and live the Christian life.

But we use the tradition with one controlling caution: we continually ask whether this or that aspect of it squares with the Bible as the Holy Spirit enables the Church to understand it. We subject every stage of tradition to the test of Scripture. This means not simply that we test the views of other Christian groups by the Bible. It means most of all that we continually ask whether our personal understanding of the gospel, and the confession and practice of our own Church, intelligently grasp and faithfully apply the Biblical message. Any Protestant who never tests or examines his own confession or that of his Church by the standard of Scripture, and who fails to keep clear that what he believes and what his Church confesses is secondary to Scripture, is a Roman Catholic at heart. He is ascribing controlling authority to his Church and its tradition.

That final control belongs to God. It is exercised by the living Christ. It is made effective in Christians by the Holy Spirit, whom Christ sent and still sends to his Church. It is centered, as far as human witness and word are concerned, in the written form of the apostolic gospel; this gospel took up the Old Testament as a witness to Christ, testified to the Church what the coming of Christ had been, and explained what that decisive act of God in Christ means for faith and Christian living. The fruitful humility of a grateful but responsible use of Christian tradition draws blessing from the Christian heritage of the Church; but it gives the final control to the working of God, who speaks his basic message to the Church through the canon of Holy Scripture by the inner witness of the Holy Spirit.

Selected Bibliography

This list of books on the canon and its place in the Church includes only works in English. Many of the best books in this field are in French and German. They will be found listed in the bibliographies of the more technical books listed below.

The Apocrypha: King James Version, with an Introduction by Robert H. Pfeiffer. Harper & Brothers, n.d.

The Apocrypha: English Revised Version (1894). Thomas Nelson & Sons, n.d.

Barth, Karl, *Church Dogmatics,* Vol. I, *The Doctrine of the Word of God,* second half-volume, tr. by G. T. Thomson and Harold Knight. Charles Scribner's Sons, 1956.

Biblical Authority for Today, ed. by Alan Richardson and W. Schweitzer. The Westminster Press, 1951.

Blackman, Edwin Cyril, *Marcion and His Influence.* S.P.C.K., London, 1948.

Brunner, Emil, *Revelation and Reason,* English translation by Olive Wyon. The Westminster Press, 1946.

Buhl, Frants, *Canon and Text of the Old Testament,* English translation by John Macpherson. T. & T. Clark, Edinburgh, 1892.

Bultmann, Rudolph, *Theology of the New Testament,* tr.

by Kendrick Grobel. Vol. II, pp. 95–142. Charles Scribner's Sons, 1955.

Charles, R. H., *The Apocrypha and Pseudepigrapha of the Old Testament in English,* Vol. I, *The Apocrypha.* Oxford: Clarendon Press, 1913.

Cullmann, Oscar, " The Plurality of the Gospels as a Theological Problem in Antiquity," tr. by S. Godman, in *The Early Church,* edited by A. J. B. Higgins. The Westminster Press, 1956.

——, " The Tradition: The Exegetical, Historical and Theological Problem," in *The Early Church,* edited by A. J. B. Higgins, pp. 55–99. The Westminster Press, 1956.

Cunliffe-Jones, Hubert, *The Authority of the Biblical Revelation.* J. Clarke & Co., London, 1945.

Dentan, Robert C., *The Apocrypha, Bridge of the Testaments.* The Seabury Press, Inc., 1954.

Dillistone, F. W., ed., *Scripture and Tradition.* Lutterworth Press, London, 1955.

Dodd, C. H., *According to the Scriptures.* Charles Scribner's Sons, 1953.

Dugmore, C. W., ed., *The Interpretation of the Bible.* S.P.C.K., London, 1944.

Farmer, Herbert H., " The Bible: Its Significance and Authority," in *The Interpreter's Bible,* Vol. I, pp. 3–31. Abingdon Press, 1952.

Goodspeed, Edgar J., *The Apocrypha: An American Translation.* University of Chicago Press, 1938.

——, *The Apostolic Fathers: An American Translation.* Harper & Brothers, 1950.

——, " The Canon of the New Testament," in *The Interpreter's Bible,* Vol. I, pp. 63–71. Abingdon Press, 1952.

——, *The Formation of the New Testament.* University of Chicago Press, 1926.

————, *New Solutions of New Testament Problems.* University of Chicago Press, 1927.

————, *The Story of the Apocrypha.* University of Chicago Press, 1939.

Harnack, Adolf von, *The Origin of the New Testament,* English translation by J. R. Wilkinson. The Macmillan Company, 1925.

James, Montague Rhodes, *The Apocryphal New Testament.* Oxford: Clarendon Press, 1924.

Jeffery, Arthur, "The Canon of the Old Testament," in *The Interpreter's Bible,* Vol. I, pp. 32–45. Abingdon Press, 1952.

Jenkins, Daniel, *Tradition and the Spirit.* Faber & Faber, Ltd., London, 1951.

Knox, John, *Marcion and the New Testament.* University of Chicago Press, 1942.

Kraeling, Emil G., *The Old Testament Since the Reformation.* Harper & Brothers, 1956.

McNeile, A. H., *An Introduction to the Study of the New Testament.* Second edition revised by C. S. C. Williams, pp. 310–372. Oxford: Clarendon Press, 1953.

Margolis, Max Leopold, *The Hebrew Scriptures in the Making.* Jewish Publication Society, 1922.

Moffatt, James, *The Thrill of Tradition.* The Macmillan Company, 1944.

Moore, George Foot, "The Definition of the Jewish Canon and the Repudiation of Christian Scriptures," in *Essays in Modern Theology and Related Subjects,* pp. 99–125. Charles Scribner's Sons, 1911.

Oesterley, W. O. E., *An Introduction to the Books of the Apocrypha.* The Macmillan Company, 1935.

Paterson, William Paterson, *The Rule of Faith.* Hodder and Stoughton, London, 1912.

Pfeiffer, Robert H., *History of New Testament Times, with an Introduction to the Apocrypha.* Harper & Brothers, 1949.

——, *Introduction to the Old Testament,* pp. 50–70. Harper & Brothers, 1941.

——, " The Literature and Religion of the Apocrypha," in *The Interpreter's Bible,* Vol. I, pp. 391–419. Abingdon Press, 1952.

Phillips, Godfrey Edward, *The Old Testament in the World Church.* Lutterworth Press, London, 1942.

Prestige, George Leonard, *Fathers and Heretics.* The Macmillan Company, 1940.

Reid, George J., " Canon of the Holy Scriptures," in *The Catholic Encyclopedia,* Vol. III, pp. 267–279. Robert Appleton Co., 1908.

Robinson, H. Wheeler, *Inspiration and Revelation in the Old Testament.* Oxford: Clarendon Press, 1946.

Rowley, H. H., *The Growth of the Old Testament.* Hutchison House, London, 1950.

——, *The Unity of the Bible.* The Westminster Press, 1955.

Ryle, Herbert Edward, *The Canon of the Old Testament.* Second edition. The Macmillan Company, 1909.

Souter, Alexander, *The Text and Canon of the New Testament.* Second edition prepared by C. S. C. Williams. Gerald Duckworth & Co., Ltd., London, 1954.

Steinmueller, John E., *A Companion to Scripture Studies,* Vol. I, pp. 44–128. Third printing. Joseph F. Wagner, 1946.

Torrey, C. C., *The Apocryphal Literature: A Brief Introduction.* Yale University Press, 1945.

Westcott, Brooke Foss, *A General Survey of the History of the Canon of the New Testament.* Seventh edition. The Macmillan Company, 1896.

Indexes

INDEX OF PASSAGES